2006

Withdrawn

What Others Are Saying ...

Television Host:

"For some families, an in-law suite is the perfect solution, and Carol's book is the perfect place to start the process."

Steve Greenberg
HGTV's Dream Builders

"In-law suites...it's a way to maintain a premium level of home care! Great information!"

Armond Budish, WKYC-TV
"Golden Opportunities" - Cleveland, OH

Media Relations Coordinator:

"With people living longer and the cost of specialized care going up, it's no surprise Klima has been getting inquiries from around the country."

Ed 'Flash' Ferenc,
Media Relations Coordinator

Building Associations:

"For those of us that have parents that are beginning to plan for their retirement home, I found it very useful and quite informative."

Brenda Callaghan, Executive Director
Greater Cleveland Chapter
(NARI) National Association
of the Remodeling Industry

"An in-law suite could fulfill many needs... these are becoming more popular, particularly because the dynamics of families are changing."

Nate Coffman,
Affairs Manager
Home Builders Association
of Greater Cleveland

Newspaper Columnist:

"Carol Klima is an inspiration to all women. The information in her book is invaluable to those seeking information on building an in-law suite. But more impressive is that she serves as a role model by creatively handling a life-changing situation in a pro-active fashion."

Kay Bryson, News Herald
Special Correspondent, Mentor, OH

Radio Show Hosts:

"This is a great concept... beneficial to everybody. You've got that privacy, that memorabilia, that independence. You can see exactly the layout you like. Great Job Carol."

Bill King,
WEOL 930AM Radio, Elyria, OH

"You provide great insight into making a home a comfortable place for the parent... for the children... you provide guidance, security and privacy. Great job."

John Jednak,
Host of 'The Home Show'
KSDO Radio
San Diego, CA

"You have made this process so easy!"

Jim McIntrye,
WDOK FM Radio, Cleveland, OH

Realtors:

"The practicality and simplicity of this book is refreshing and long overdue."

Art Volpe, Realty One
Greater Cleveland, OH

What People Like You Are Saying ...

"We enjoyed your first book and are eagerly looking forward to this one. Thank you for specifically addressing the issues of cohabitation with your children!"

Donald & Shirley Taylor
Medina, OH

"My daughter and I have talked about this for the last several years. After reading the article in the News Herald, I knew it was the answer to a prayer. Thank you for a great book."

Patricia S. Clude
Medina, OH

"We retrieved a lot of valuable information. Thank you for writing that book!"

Heidi & Jim Gorgan
Riverview, FL

"My mother called me one day raving about this book. Thank you for sharing your wisdom and experience with us."

Lynda Lowery
Bridgeman, MI

"The book was very helpful... much information that covers all aspects of planning your future with family. Thank you so much!"

Cooper family & Carol Messit
Grafton, OH

"My architect is also excited about receiving a copy of your book. Congratulations on an important job beautifully done!"

Marge Glaser
Cincinnati, OH

"Seeing the article in the Tampa Tribune was a message from God to me. Thanks for sharing this valuable information."

Mary Fernandez
Tampa, FL

"Thanks for all your efforts, ideas, and drive; making a trying, time consuming project so much easier!"

Dianna Rockey
Appleton, WI

"Your cheerfulness helps take away some of the dread that accompanies leaving our comfortable living for something entirely new, but quite necessary."

J. H. Taggart
Avon Park, FL

"Much praise to you for putting forth the efforts to write your books that will definitely help others. Thanks again."

Peggy Staples
Lighthouse Point, FL

"My husband and I are eager to use this [book] to help us with our changing family needs."

Candace C. Monforton
Dade City, FL

"I so appreciate your efforts in putting this well needed publication together. I know it's going to make my life a little easier and I'm sure I'll be able to adapt one of your many plans to our specific needs."

Debbie Banks
Columbia, SC

Build Your Own
IN-LAW SUITE
- Floor Plans & More!

by: Carol J. Klima

Fourth Edition

Homestead Press

396 Fairwood Circle
Berea, OH 44017

1-888-769-6335

Build Your Own IN-LAW SUITE
- Floor Plans & More!

by Carol J. Klima

PUBLISHED BY:

Homestead Press
396 Fairwood Circle
Berea, OH 44017

Printed in Canada

ISBN 0-9672207-5-0

Library of Congress PCN
2004102985

Table of Contents

Dedication

*A special thank you to all my family and friends who
helped and encouraged me through my new adventure.*

*Leslie Krupman, Becky Demitro, Cara Proehl
Karen Hesseltine, Kathy Drake, Hazel Drake
Gloria Lee & my husband Dale*

Introduction

Our Parents Are Living Longer!

The twenty-first century has been met by a tremendous increase in the number of elderly, thus causing a great need for affordable housing and personal care for those in their senior years. The children from the baby booming years of the past century are now nearing retirement age. They face many decisions that need to be made concerning not only their own future, but the future of their aging parents as well. Many elderly will have to make living adjustments in the near future, making these decisions themselves or through the aid of their children.

It may become impossible for our parents to maintain their house and property that they have lived in for so many years. They will no doubt find that their life-style has to be simplified and the amount of possessions reduced. The children may want to eliminate more items than their parents are willing to part with. Seeing their belongings boxed up and carried out the door may cause the parent a great deal of emotional stress, yet they are no longer capable of caring for these unnecessary things.

According to the 'World Health Organization' those 60 and older will number over a billion by the year 2020

Change can be Difficult!

To make a change in later years can be very traumatic for some, while others may have no problem adjusting to a move at all. This is when the children may need to help guide the parents in the right direction, offering suggestions, and helping the parent to see how this change could be the best possible solution to their problem. How can we help our parents adapt to a new residence, a new life-style, give them the care they need, and make this change as smooth and easy as possible? This could be a challenge but is not impossible!

Financial Issues may be Involved

Various types of assisted living facilities, retirement communities, and nursing homes are being constructed throughout the United States to accommodate the growing number of elderly. When families check into the cost of these above mentioned facilities, they discover the fees add up to considerable amounts of money; especially when it comes to the need for long-term care. Even if you have insurance coverage you may find that they will pay for only a limited time in these facilities. This is prompting many families to consider home care, making it a popular choice around the country.

This can be a very stressful time for the adult children as well. They would like the parents to have the very best care, but the parents' financial situation may not allow the nicer options. The children may not be able to afford these facilities either. Which option will be affordable and still give the parent the care and independence they desire?

Who Will Take Responsibility?

An important question is, will the other siblings help with the expenses and personal care needed? Sometimes siblings can't come to an agreement as to what arrangements to make for housing their aging parents. You and your immediate family may be the only ones willing to take on the responsibility of caring for your parents. The fact that some in the family may not want to deal with the situation at all, adds even more pressure and stress to an already emotional time.

Many are finding the best care can be right in their own home and prove to be something more affordable. When personal care is needed, who are in the best position to give that care? This point needs to be considered. Many elderly are quite independent,

but just find it difficult to maintain a house and the surrounding property. There are others who are plagued with many health problems that make daily living difficult. Most seniors are on a fixed income and may just need an affordable place to live and a minimum amount of help. Whatever their needs, it will most likely be up to the children to resolve these problems for their parents.

Separate but Close-by

An in-law suite is separate. Some today have a parent living in the same house with them. Likely the parent would prefer to have a separate, private area to reside. The in-law suite could fill this need. It can be a small area, or a completely self-contained suite with a kitchen and laundry area. This option allows both the children's family and the parent to maintain their privacy and still be close enough to give immediate help when necessary. We all tend to be creatures of habit. A separate area helps to eliminate opinion conflicts over small things and causes less friction.

If you are trying to buy a house with an in-law suite already attached, you will most likely find out that they are very expensive, if you can find them at all. There is a good market for houses with an in-law suite. You might be able to add on to either your current home or one you plan to purchase. If buying another property, be sure to check with the building department of that city concerning requirements before making your purchase. Make sure the type of structure you desire is allowed in the community.

Talking Out the Details

The children may be planning ahead for the parent to eventually move into the main house with them. As time passes, the parent may need more help but doesn't want

Sit down and patiently discuss the needs of your loved ones

to bother the rest of the family or impose his or her problems on the children. If the family could just sit down together and discuss the exact needs, they may find this in-law suite option the answer to a lot of problems.

In many cases elderly ones don't want to make a change until they are desperate to do so. Often a lot of the decision making then falls on the shoulders of the children, whereas the parent would actually have preferred to make these decisions themselves. It might be wiser and easier to make a change sooner than waiting until worsening health conditions compound existing problems.

Talking openly concerning the financial arrangements, who's paying for certain items, is the best way to resolve the problem of money. Some parents may have enough money to pay for the construction of their suite; others may need the children to foot the bill. Everyone's circumstances will be different and may need to be discussed many times before the problem is resolved. If the children want to include the cost of the suite in their existing house payment, they may want to refinance. Of course, it would be better to do this at a time when interest rates are lower.

Advantages of the In-Law Suite can be Many

Check the list on the next page to see what would apply to your situation. This will enable you to make a sound decision concerning your family's needs.

The adult children should discuss the list with the parent. Reassure mom or dad that this option could make their own responsibility of parent care easier too.

"If you choose to pursue this course, I wish you much success and happiness".

Carol J. Klima

Advantages of the In-law Suite:

For Elderly Parents:

Avoid high-cost facilities

Maintain independence

Feel secure

Retain own possessions

May keep pet

Emotional support from family

Alleviates loneliness

Easier to clean and maintain

Family cares for lawn and snow removal

Help near for meals, medication, and laundry

Normal life-style, less worry

Grandchildren near (fringe benefit!)

Financial help

No inside steps

No accidental lock out (family has spare key)

Physical help from family as opposed to strangers

Comfort to know children inherit

Not intruding on family's privacy

Children maintain structure

Advantages of the In-law Suite:

For Adult Children:

Knowing parent(s) safe

No time consuming trips to help parents

Convenient to make daily checks

Are they eating properly?

Are they taking their medications?

Easier to do laundry

No guilt feelings of not doing enough

Eliminate the maintaining of two properties

You set a good example for your children to follow

Adds value to property

Can oversee in-home health care workers

Parent may watch grandchildren

Someone to watch house, feed pets, etc.

May someday use suite yourself

Protect parent(s) from con artists

Easier to run errands

Make sure the bills are paid

Saves money

Peace of mind

Avoid Mistakes; Save Time and Money

If you are considering adding an in-law suite to your home, we feel that the following information will be of value to you, giving you many useful and practical ideas to consider. We started to become involved in building our in-law suite when it became obvious to us that we needed to make changes in our life-style. Through trial, error, and much effort, we were able to complete our project.

The purpose of this book is to help others avoid some common mistakes, cut costs, and save time on the planning of your in-law suite.

When we were in the process of building our in-law suite, we were able to keep expenses down in a number of ways. One way was by obtaining the building permit by ourselves. In our community, building permits are less expensive if the homeowner acquires the permit.

The one who acquires the building permit is considered the contractor and is responsible for city codes being properly followed. He is also liable for any injuries on the building site!

One or more walk-in closets are welcome additions to an in-law suite. If the one who will be living in the suite is handicapped, lower hanger rods and shelves. Consider installing see-thru clear shelving. Also add extra hooks at lower levels for their convenience.

Builders usually charge by the square foot. Practical floor plans with no wasted space will allow you to have larger rooms and cuts down on construction costs. Many floor plans contained in this publication do not have hallways, thus, all the space is well utilized.

We were also able to save money by doing some of the work ourselves, and by having relatives and friends lend a hand. We realize not everyone knows enough people who are in the building trades, and therefore, cannot cut expenses in this manner. If there is any way that you can recruit others to lend a hand, by all means do so. This will alleviate some of the expenses associated with building an addition.

Choose the basic floor plan you like. If you want to make any modifications on your chosen floor plan, just show it to the contractor and he will be able to make the adjustments. You can make rooms larger or smaller, as well as change the overall size of the suite to accommodate attachment to the main house.

Specific ways we cut expenses:

- Hanging and taping the drywall. Our son is a drywall taper.

- Staining and varnishing the woodwork. This job is more involved than what you might think. It's a lot of work!

- Painting the interior. Don't forget that the new drywall needs to be coated with a special primer before painting.

- Roof. Shingles are very heavy items. You may want to consider using a supplier who makes what is called 'roof top' deliveries. This is a lesson we learned the hard way. Get as much help as possible, it's a very big job.

- Windows. We purchased new windows from a manufacturer at half the price. We were able to save money on these windows because they were mismeasured from other jobs. Your carpenter will know how to make the windows fit.

- Flooring. Another way that we were able to save money was on the installation of the carpeting and linoleum. Thankfully, we have relatives in that business.

- Jacks. Run the telephone and cable wires before the drywall goes up. A friend of ours has the know-how to install telephone jacks. Put in plenty of jacks in all the rooms because circumstances change.

- Light fixtures. We went to a close-out store and watched for sales.

- Plumbing fixtures. We saved money by comparing prices. We even found a perfectly good stainless steel sink at a garage sale. Your choice of certain materials will affect the total cost of the project. Sinks, faucets, and light fixtures can vary greatly in price.

- Materials. Your choice of certain materials will affect the total cost of the project. Sinks, faucets, and light fixtures can vary greatly in price. Choose moderately priced fixtures if you need to be cost conscience. Keep in mind that fixtures cheaply made, may need to be replaced after a relatively short time.

Choosing a Contractor

Check References

- When looking for a contractor, ask friends and relatives for their recommendations. Check with the Better Business Bureau (BBB) or the National Association of the Remodeling Industry (NARI) in your local area.

- There are many reputable smaller builders who specialize in additions and take a great deal of pride in their work. Smaller builders may be more inclined to work with you to keep costs down without sacrificing quality. Our contractor had no problem in allowing us to do some of the work. Remember to get several bids before you proceed.

- Make sure the contractor is licensed and bonded! This is very important and can save you a lot of headaches in the future.

You can save money by having family and friends help with some of the finish work

Have a Written Contract

- Get everything in writing! The contract should include the warranty, dates for payments and construction, and any other pertinent information.

- Contractors will usually give a one year limited warranty on the materials and labor used in your in-law suite.

- Some contractors allow you to do some of the work but continue to charge you the same price for the job. In other words, you are saving nothing by doing things yourself.

- Your contract should state the time the work commences and when it should be completed. Remember that unforeseen circumstances or problems, such as weather, may cause short delays.

- To avoid any problems or misunderstandings, ask for an itemized estimate for each step of the building process, like the sample on the next page.

- If you think the total price is a little too high, check the cost of each item listed. Sometimes you can negotiate a better price on a certain item, such as the plumbing or electrical work. Perhaps you can save several hundred dollars. It's worth the effort.

Sample Estimate

Escavating & Rough Grade	$2,400.00
Water & Gas Lines	$950.00
Footer & Foundation	$3,500.00
Concrete Work & Fill	$3,450.00
Sidewalk	$700.00
Rough Carpentry	$5,000.00
Electrical	$2,500.00
Plumbing	$5,250.00
Heating & Air Conditioning	$3,500.00
Drywall	$2,250.00
Insulation	$1,200.00
Siding, Gutters, Downspouts	$3,750.00
Kitchen Cabinets & Vanity	$2,550.00
Interior Trim	$1,400.00
Flooring	$2,250.00
Interior Painting	$2,000.00
TOTAL	$42,650.00*

* This is only a sample of some of the prices a builder might charge, and does not necessarily reflect what the final cost of your in-law suite will be!

Paying the Contractor

- *Never* pay the builder the entire amount up front - and neither should your bank!

- Contractors are generally paid in four (4) installments. This protects you, and allows the contractor enough money to continue the job, to buy materials, and to pay his employees.

The down payment will generally be about **10 - 15%** of the total cost, depending where you live and the terms you and the contractor agree to.

The second payment is usually required after the footer and slab is completed.

The third payment is made upon completion of the 'rough-in' work. This would include water, sewer, and gas lines.

The fourth and final payment is not made until the completion of the project and a walk-through inspection is made with the contractor. Only when you are completely satisfied will you make the final payment.

For Your Safety

Security

- Generally, building codes require more than one access door into and out of your in-law suite, especially for a self-contained suite. That is why in my larger floor plans I incorporate patio doors in the bedrooms as a safety feature in case of fire. Also, during warmer weather a patio door can provide more air and light. You can also install a regular door somewhere else in the suite. What you decide will depend on the layout of the in-law suite and the way it is attached to the main house.

- Install an outside light that has a motion sensor on it. The light will turn on when anyone approaches in the dark. This will help prevent falls and fumbling with keys when entering.

- Dead bolt locks are recommended by law enforcement agencies for security purposes. You might want to give an extra set of keys to your relatives in the main house, or perhaps you can leave a key with a trusted neighbor just in case of an emergency. Avoid the kind of dead bolt locks that require a key to unlock the door from the inside. This could cause unnecessary delays when exiting the in-law suite during a fire or some other kind of emergency. It would be good to install some type of extra protection such as a "charlie bar" on the patio door to deter unsavory characters.

Rafter-truss tie

or

"Hurricane clip"

- There are many different types of door handles to choose from. Select the kind of handle that will make it easier for the occupant to use. For instance, a person with arthritis may not want a round door knob because it will be more difficult to turn. Instead, they might prefer a lever handle. Handles on pocket doors could be awkward for some older people, but the pocket door might be easier for a person in a wheelchair to enter and exit a room.

- A peephole in the entrance door will allow the occupant to safely see if there are any unwanted visitors. While installing the peephole, don't forget to consider the height of the occupant.

Fire, Wind, & Smoke

- If your in-law suite is connected to an attached garage, you may want to install a fire door between the suite and the garage. This can provide easy access to your automobile during bad weather, and allow quick access to your relatives.

- Many communities require the use of rafter-truss ties or hurricane clips. They attach to the roof and the walls during construction. Even if your city code doesn't mandate them, install them anyway. They may prevent your roof from blowing away during high winds. They are inexpensive and easy to install.

- Fire codes mandate that fire rated drywall be on all walls that connect to a garage. Generally, this is 5/8" thick drywall. Your contractor can give you more details in this regard.

- Smoke and carbon monoxide detectors are very important. Many communities require them. The type of detector that is powered by electricity will also need batteries to function properly. By having a smoke detector and a fire extinguisher, you may be able to save money on your insurance premiums. The smoke detector should not be installed too close to the kitchen. This will keep the detector from sounding an alarm every time you use a skillet.

- In some parts of the country, radon gas is a concern, usually homes with basements. If you are worried about this, you can get a detector that will identify the presence of this gas.

Smoke, carbon monoxide, and radon detectors can save lives

Water Heaters, Furnaces, and Electricity

- Give attention to the temperature setting on the hot water tank. Older people do not react as fast as they once did, and because of this, they could suffer a severe burn if the setting is too hot.

- Use only 'ground fault interrupter' (GFI) electrical outlets in the kitchen and bathroom. They can help prevent accidental shock and may save your loved one from a severe injury due to circuit overload or dropping an electrical appliance into a sink full of water.

- Another area that you might give attention to is what kind of range to install in you kitchen. In some mobile home parks and in some retirement apartments only electric ranges are allowed. This is because older people sometimes forget to turn off the gas burners and create a fire hazard. This is not to say that electric ranges are safer. You are the one that must decide which one best fits your needs.

- You and your contractor will have to determine if your in-law suite will need its own separate furnace and hot water tank. Whether they are needed or not will depend on whether the units in the main house can accommodate the extra load. At one point in the planning stage we considered putting our furnace and hot water tank in the basement of the main house rather than in the in-law suite. For us this was not practical because of the limited access to the basement from the in-law suite. Your builder can help you determine what best suits the structure's layout.

Emergency Alert

- It would be good to install a special pull-cord in the bathroom to alert family members or other emergency service providers to a medical crisis. When there is a need, time is of the essence.

- Grab bars should be installed parallel to the floor for proper balance for the user. Towel racks should not be used as grab bars. They are not made for this purpose and can break when too much weight is applied.

Miscellaneous Tips

Financing an Addition

- If you have to borrow money for this addition, check with your city and county for any low interest home improvement loans. Some communities have programs designed to help their residents upgrade their property.

Saving Money

- Use moderately priced fixtures. If you choose fixtures that are cheaply made, you will most likely have to replace them after a short period of time.

Paint and Wallcovering

- Wallcovering can add charm and beauty to your in-law suite. If you need to cut costs, you may want to paint your walls. I suggest latex paint with a satin finish because it can be easily cleaned and doesn't have the high gloss that enamel paints possess. Lighter colors can brighten a room and tend to make rooms appear larger. Other methods you might consider using are, the two colored paint rollers, or the rag and sponge application method. This will give your walls the look of having a wallcovering pattern at a much lower cost. Check your local paint store for the latest ideas in home decorating. Borders around the top of your walls will give your room a finished touch and will add contrasting colors to enhance your decor.

Noise Reduction

- Since in-law suites tend to be small, it may be worth the expense to soundproof the bathroom and furnace room walls. You can use insulation as soundproofing, but it will not reduce sound as much as regular soundproofing. We did this and it has been well worth the effort. When doing the laundry, I shut the door to the bathroom and I can hardly hear the noise made by the washer and dryer.

- Another thing that can help in keeping down noise is purchasing quiet-running appliances. We chose a Maytag® dishwasher because of this feature. Choose whatever fits your needs and your budget.

- You can also install a commode that flushes quietly and quickly.

Ceilings

- Vaulted ceilings can add the look of spaciousness to a room. The major drawback is that it becomes more expensive to heat the room. Heat rises collecting in the peaks of the ceiling, causing the need for more warm air to be forced into the room. Eight-foot ceilings will keep an elderly person warmer without adding to your heating bill. If you live in a colder climate, lower ceilings are the better choice.

Lights

- Some contractors don't automatically install ceiling lights in the bedrooms. Good lighting in all the rooms is very practical, as many elderly experience  eye problems. When dressing or putting on their cosmetics, dim lights can be very annoying. Low lighting could also cause accidental tripping and injury. The contractor might think that lamps in a bedroom are more stylish, or they might be cutting installation cost for more profit. Let your contractor know your needs ahead of time.

*Higher ceilings
waste heat*

*Ceiling fans
are economical*

Fans

- A ceiling fan with a light fixture might be preferred. The joist above the drywall should be reinforced to hold the added weight of the fan. Even if you're not putting a fan in at the time of construction, you may decide to install one at a later date. A fan with five blades will give a better air flow. Ceiling fans can save you money on your cooling costs. You can even run them while the air conditioner is on.

Extra Support Around Windows

- One thing you may want to do is attach extra pieces of wood between the studs above the windows and the patio door before the drywall is installed. This will help you when hanging curtains and drapes by giving you something solid for the screws to be secured into. Rods attached with only nails may not be strong enough to hold heavier window treatments. When you open and close a traverse rod, stress can cause screws to become loose and even come out of the wall. When there is only drywall for support, you can use toggle bolts or hollow wall fasteners to anchor curtain rods to the wall.

Traverse rods and vertical blinds need more support

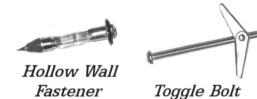

Hollow Wall Fastener   *Toggle Bolt*

Record Stud Placement

- Before the drywall is hung and the studs are hidden, you may want to make a sketch as to the placement of the wall studs and the measurements between them. Keep this information in a safe place for future reference. When your suite is finished, you will be able to find the studs quickly for hanging heavy objects and avoid making unnecessary holes in the wall that will need to be repaired. Grab bars may have to be installed now or at a later date. Knowing the stud placement around the shower, commode, or on a bedroom wall, will be very beneficial. You can also install extra wood supports around these areas prior to the hanging of the drywall so you will have something very solid to attach the grab bars to.

- Remember, the dimensions on my floor plans are centerline measurements. This means that you lose a few inches in each room. Your contractor will know how to make the necessary adjustments. Room sizes can be made larger or smaller depending on your needs. Discuss this with your contractor before construction starts.

Discuss room size changes with your contractor

Ideas for the Bathroom

Plan Ahead

- How you design the bathroom in your in-law suite will depend a lot on who will be living there. How old are they? How mobile are they? Do they need a shower with wheelchair access? These questions and a host of others need to be addressed before you even begin the final design of the bathroom. It is easier and less expensive to install fixtures that may be needed in the future now, than trying to remodel later.

Vanity and Mirror

- Our bathroom vanity matches our kitchen cabinets; therefore it is up a little higher than a regular vanity. This could be an advantage for one who is tall or has severe back problems. It isn't necessary for the bathroom vanity to have the same finish as your kitchen cabinets. There are many different styles to choose from that are reasonably priced. A backsplash surrounding the countertop will help prevent splatters on the lower part of the mirror.

- A medicine cabinet with a three-way mirror will add more storage for sundries. We found this to be a great advantage for the two of us.

Double sinks can be added to some of the larger bathrooms

Sinks and Faucets

- We've found that single-handled faucets are easier to use. Dual-handled faucets, especially those with round handles, are often difficult to turn on and off when your hands are wet. They may be attractive but sometimes they can be impractical. Eldery people often have arthritis or loss of strength in their hands and find it difficult to turn round knobs and open tight drawers.

- Pedestal sinks are very attractive and stylish. Keep in mind, that you will lose drawer and storage space by not installing a vanity. Will the occupant have difficulties cleaning the floor around the pedestal base?

Bathtubs and Showers

- Those who find it difficult to step into a bathtub would do well to install a shower stall. Some contain seats that can aid a person with disabilities. You may want to consider a shower with a barrier free floor which is made for easy wheelchair access.

- Choose shower doors that are easy to clean. Some doors overlap and are difficult to clean without removing them. Sliding doors have tracks that tend to accumulate dirt buildup. The shower shown here has a door that swings out and is easy to clean. Perhaps just a shower curtain will suit your needs.

- Water controls for the shower or tub areas can be offset on the wall for easier use. This may prevent accidents, such as scalding and falls.

- An elderly person may prefer a hand-held shower that removes from the wall bracket for a sit down shower in a bathtub.

- Whirlpool bathtubs can be helpful in easing some health conditions. Consider whether the one who will be using it is capable of getting into and out of the tub without assistance.

This shower stall seat is installed to fold down as needed

- A shower or tub should have a slip resistant floor surface.

Commode

- An elongated and elevated commode may be easier to use than the standard size. Only a narrow shelf can be used behind it, because the seat is longer and won't stay up for cleaning or usage if the shelf is too wide.

- For a wheelchair occupant it would be good to consider rearranging the bathroom for easier access to the commode and other features. Check the various floor plans to get ideas that will work for you.

Grab Bars & Hooks

- A grab bar installed by the commode may be needed by some. If so, have wood reinforcement in the wall before the drywall is installed to assure a solid attachment. Grab bars may also be needed in shower or tub areas as well.

- Put up clothing hooks on backs of doors, in closets, and particularly next to the shower or bathtub. They can prevent one from reaching too far for a towel and falling. Many accidental falls at home occur in the bathtub or the shower. You can lower the towel racks for those confined in a wheelchair.

- Pocket doors slide into the wall and out of the way. These doors might be easier for a person in a wheelchair to use. Keep in mind that pocket door handles can be more difficult to use if the person has arthritis in the hands or fingers. If a regular bathroom door is used, it should not swing inward.

Slip-resistant Flooring

- A slip-resistant linoleum floor is another safety feature you might want to consider because it can prevent serious injuries from accidental falls.

Combined Laundry Facilities

- Will the occupant be doing his or her own laundry? The answer will determine whether or not you need a washer and dryer in their in-law suite. If not, you can make the bathroom smaller, or use the extra space for storage by installing more cabinets or closets.

- If you decide to install a standard washer and dryer in the bathroom, you will benefit by installing cabinets above them to hold your detergent, softener, and other items you will need to launder your clothes. Other supplies can be stored in this cabinet as well.

Bathroom Windows

- In our in-law suite, we installed a small awning style window in the bathroom. This allows light to shine in. For privacy, you may want to have frosted glass in the window. As I mentioned earlier, we purchased mis-measured windows. Because of this our bathroom did not have the frosted glass we wanted. To solve this problem, we went to a home improvement store and bought a roll of Rubbermaid Frosted Contact Paper to cover the glass. It looks like the real thing and was inexpensive!

- City code may require a certain height for the bathroom window if it does not contain some sort of safety glass. Our window had to be 5' from the floor to the bottom of the window. We actually prefer this height because it allows us to open the window in nice weather and enjoy a cooling breeze and privacy.

Ideas For The Kitchen

Refrigerators

- Allow a refrigerator space of 36 inches wide and 70 inches high. This will accommodate a 21 or 22 cubic foot refrigerator with a little room to spare. By allowing this size space, you will have enough room should you purchase a large unit in the future.

- In smaller kitchens, side-by-side refrigerator doors are more practical and convenient to open and close. When the refrigerator is against a side wall, make sure the unit door can fully open. You can adjust the size of the entrance to the kitchen to accomplish this. Otherwise, some of the drawers will not be able to slide in and out.

- Do not place a refrigerator directly against a heat source, such as a range or a dishwasher. In many cases, the range and the refrigerator are on the same side of the kitchen. A counter space between the two appliances, as shown in the picture to the right, eliminates the problem.

Do not place a refrigerator next to a heat source

Ranges and Microwave Ovens

- A two-burner range costing from $150 - $250 can be used for very small areas, like kitchenettes. This kind of range has only a front and back burner with no oven.

- An apartment dishwasher is about half the size of a standard dishwasher.

- You may want some type of back-splash around your counter sink top. This is usually easier to clean, protects the lower part of the wall, and looks attractive. Tile or wallpaper may be preferred, but will also cost more. Tile would prevent you from hanging measuring spoons, steak knives, hand cooking utensils, etc.

- Installing an over-the-range microwave ovenhood will free up counter space. Check city code on the height allowance. The lower you install the microwave the more room there will be for a cabinet. This will also make it easier for an elderly person to reach.

Countertops and Cabinets

- U-shaped cabinet handles make doors and drawers easier to open. Many elderly persons experience problems with hands and fingers, making the simplest task a struggle. To prevent clothing from getting caught, don't install the type of handle that has an overhang on the sides. Some prefer no handles at all. The cabinets are easier to clean with no handles, but it will be harder to open the doors and drawers.

- The space above the cabinets may be left open to set plants, decorative cookie jars, etc. Others may prefer to have a soffit above their cabinets. If you want more storage in the kitchen you can install cabinets that go up to the ceiling, to put items that are seldom used. Consider whether the elderly parent will be climbing too high to retrieve items. This could lead to a fall and very serious injuries.

- Corner cabinets are hard to use because items tend to get pushed way back in the corner and are hard to reach. Install a lazy susan for easier access.

Sinks and Disposals

- A stainless steel sink may be advisable because ceramic sinks are more prone to chip when something is dropped in them.

- The kitchen sink can be situated close to the pantry as in suite #24, which allows for larger cabinets. Your builder or cabinet dealer will help you plan the layout that will be practical for the amount of space you have.

- Smooth surface countertops are easier to clean than a porous surface or ceramic tile.

- A garbage disposal switch should be far enough away to prevent accidents by having one's hand in the disposal drain while trying to retrieve an item that may have fallen into the disposal. The best rule is, *never* put your hand into a garbage disposal! Purchase a disposal that has a restart key or button. A cheap disposal may give you problems.

Pantries and Windows

- The kitchen pantry is good for storage. If the shelves are set back a few inches from the door, you will have space to set a broom or mop inside. A narrow shelf on the top will give extra space for rarely used items. Wire or plastic racks may be installed on the inside of the door for light items like plastic bags, wax paper, spices, etc.

- Install a window in the kitchen for natural lighting and to save on electricity. A small kitchen will get very warm when cooking and baking. A window can be opened to ventilate the area when an exhaust fan might not be enough air flow.

Handicapped Accessibility

If the occupant is in a wheelchair, or may need one at a later date, it may be wise to install larger doors. This will allow more mobility for the person in a wheelchair, and in the long run save you money and aggravation by not having to modify later. Entrance doors are usually 36 inches wide.

- If a wheelchair ramp is needed, you can save money by installing it during construction, especially if the ramp is made of concrete. Wooden ramps can be installed at a later date. Portable ramps are now available for temporary use.

- Install flooring that will make maneuvering a wheelchair easier. A shorter napped or commercial carpet may be preferable for durability and ease of movement.

- The bathroom door should not swing inward for a person in a wheelchair because it makes access more difficult. Interior doors should be at least 36 inches wide.

- Those in a wheelchair need to have the thermostat, wall switches, cabinets, clothing rods, hooks, and towel racks lower for easier access.

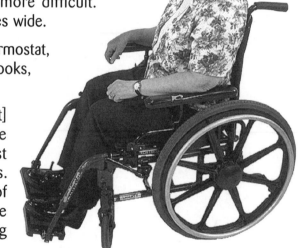

There are many ADA [American Disability Act] approved fixtures for the convenience and welfare of persons in a wheelchair. Some items may cost more, but may be necessary for certain individuals. The following list is intended to make you aware of their availability and possible choices. More information can be obtained at your local building supply stores. Compare for quality and price!

Ramp:
- Ramp to main entrance should be at least 3 feet wide with railings
- Install non-slip surface on ramp and landing
- Landings should be 5 feet square for easy turn-around

Windows:
- Easy open with locks
- Lower height of bathroom window requires safety glass

Ceiling Fan:
- Remote control fan and light

Doors:

- 36 inch wide entrance door
- Second access door must also be 36 inches wide
- Threshold - beveled ¼ inch
- Lever handles
- Inside doors - 36 inch wide
- A pocket door slides into the wall out of the way
  This type of door may be more expensive to install
- The bathroom door should not swing inward
- Some disabled people prefer no interior doors at all
- Do not install a storm door

Lights:

- Automatic outdoor sensor light
- Inside - lower height for wall switches
- Easy touch switch pads
- Automatic indoor motion sensor lights

Room sizes:

- An 11 x 12 foot bedroom may be sufficient, but a larger size would be better
- Install a grab bar on the wall next to the bed
- Choose a larger bathroom floor plan for easy maneuvering
- Kitchen needs at least 49-50 inches of middle floor space

Thermostat:

- Place thermostat lower on the wall for easier reach

Closet:

- Hanging pole fixtures and shelving should be lowered
- See-thru clear shelving makes it easier to find items
- Extra hooks for convenience

Flooring:

- Non-slip linoleum or tile in bathroom and kitchen
- Low nap carpeting (commercial type more durable)

Bathroom:

- Water mixing valve - thermostat retains water at a safe temperature. Most showers now have this protection
- Lower clothing hooks and towel racks
- Mirror should be low enough for the occupant yet high enough for a guest, or tilt on a downward angle
- Handicap sinks - firmly attach to walls. Insulate plumbing underneath sink to avoid burns
- Lever handle or single-handle fixtures (no round knobs)
- Water tight dome light above shower
- Emergency pull-cord to alert family emergency services
- Shower stall - barrier free, non-slip (Some have a raised edge that can be converted at a later date) Compare prices
- Grab bars installed horizontally or vertically, never at an angle. Some have an easy grip surface
- Folding grab bars with hinge locks
- Shower fixture can be offset - closer to entrance
- Shower with built-in molded seats. Pull-down seats can be padded, wood, or custom made
- Soap and shampoo bottle holders
- Use a shower curtain rather than a glass door
- Bathtub or shower with non-slip bottom
- Choose a floor plan with larger bathroom floor space for easier wheelchair maneuvering

Insulate pipes under sink

Install grab bars on wall next to toilet and on back wall

Commode:

- Elevated, 18 inches or same height as a wheelchair
- Right-handed flushing toilets
- Elongated seat for one who is taller or has a larger build
- Allow 32 to 36 inches open space on the side of toilet
- Non-sweating toilet tanks, avoids water puddles on the floor
- Wall-hung handicap urinal with height suggestions

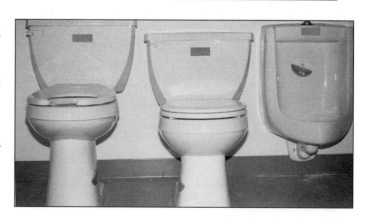

Kitchen:

- Stainless steel handicap sink with 5 to 6 inch bowl depth - insulate exposed plumbing
- Purchase a fixture with a height adjustment for filling large containers. It is desirable for a suite that has no utility tub
- Side-by-side refrigerators have smaller doors for easier access
- Wheelchair footrests need a clearance of about 10 inches high and 8 inches deep for cabinets
- You can get cabinets with pullout trays, racks, and cutting boards
- See-through drawers, shelving, and lazy susan
- Small microwave on counter top for accessibility
- Use a range with front control knobs
- A two burner range can be turned sideways for easier use

Laundry Area:

- Front-loading clothes washer and dryer with easy access front control knobs
- Washer and dryer shut-off valves with lower, easy access
- Drop down ironing board that attaches to the wall
- Lower utility tub, clothes hanging rods, hooks, shelves, cabinets, and towel racks
- Easy reach for GFI outlets
- 220 line for electric dryer
- Gas line for gas dryer
- Lower electrical breaker box

Your Local Building Department
The building department where you live may have requirements such as the following:

Getting a Building Permit

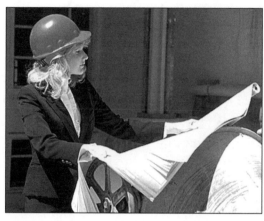

- A building permit is necessary before starting your addition. Keep in mind that there is a time limit on most building permits. This means that you must start and complete your project within a given time; do not apply for the permit too soon.

- Building permits may be less expensive if the homeowner acquires the permit rather than having the builder do it. A word of warning! If you decide to get the permit yourself, *you* are considered the contractor and are responsible for making sure that building codes are properly followed. In addition, *you* are liable for any injuries incurred by anyone working on the project! If you do not want to accept this responsibility, it would be better to have your contractor obtain the building permit because he should have workman's compensation insurance for his employees. If family and friends are doing part of the work, the contractor may wish you to acquire the permit.

The Property Survey

- Usually when an addition is built, the building department will stipulate that a recent survey of the property be provided before they will issue a building permit. A survey can cost from $350 to over $1,000. If you have recently moved into your home, you might ask the bank or mortgage company for a copy of the survey that was done when you purchased your home. Your local building department will inform you of what will be needed.

- Most communities have rules as to how close a structure can be to your property line and to your neighbor's house. Our city required us to be ten feet from the property line. Because of this, it necessitated a change in our floor plan from the one we originally wanted to build. A variance might be granted by the city, but this can be a long drawn-out process. We found it best to make changes in our design.

Will You Need a Blueprint?

- The building department we dealt with accepted our floor plan (Suite #24), making a blueprint unnecessary.

- The building inspector did want a 3-D view of the roof to show how the water would drain off. To keep from having to hire an architect, we made a rough drawing that was accepted (See page 25). If you are not able to do this yourself, perhaps your contractor will be able to help you with a rough sketch.

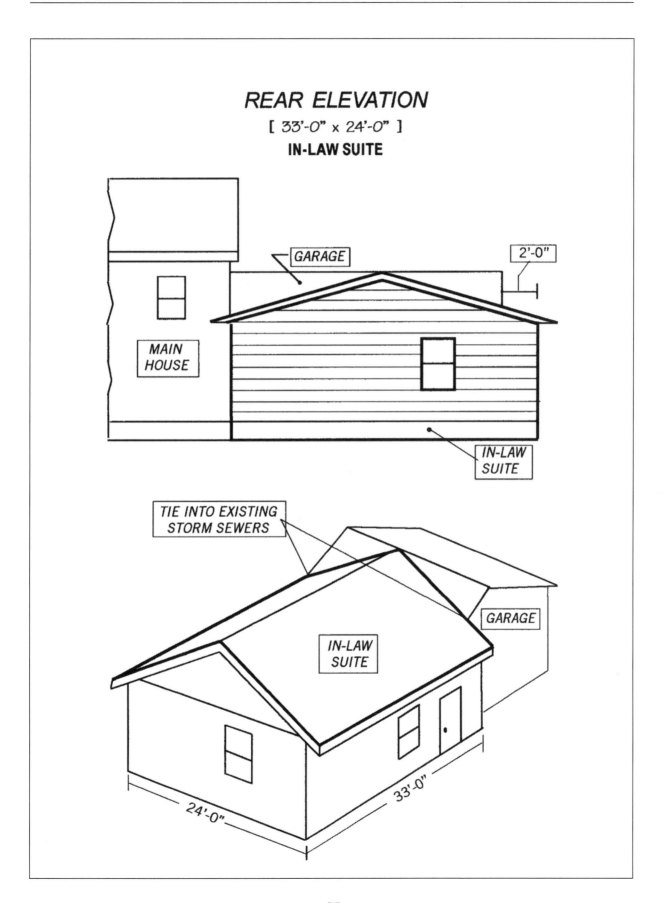

REAR ELEVATION
[33'-0" x 24'-0"]
IN-LAW SUITE

GARAGE

2'-0"

MAIN
HOUSE

IN-LAW
SUITE

TIE INTO EXISTING
STORM SEWERS

IN-LAW
SUITE

GARAGE

24'-0"

33'-0"

Maintaining Single-Family Building Classification

- Some communities require a shared living space. The suite would have a door with direct access into the main house sharing a kitchen, family room, or possibly a utility room. This also prevents the owners from turning the suite into a rental property. Cities want to keep these properties as single-family dwellings with only family members living in them. Even a self-contained addition will likely keep this status.

- When a kitchen is not allowed, some people rename this space as a computer room, sewing room, or a storage area, and hope that at a later date they will be allowed to install a kitchen. Discuss this with your contractor.

- Taxes will be included with the main house as a single family dwelling.

- Cable is with the main house also. A special box connection may be needed.

Utilities

- All utilities are often required to be on one meter with the main house, keeping the property as a single-family dwelling. This also hinders a new owner from turning the suite into a rental property in the event you sell at a later date. A suite with a furnace can have its own thermostat for heat and air control.

- Gas, water, and sewer lines in rooms that are closely situated to the main house helps to lower the cost of materials and installation.

Roofing

- It may be a good idea to have your roofer install a "water underlayment." This stops water leakage caused by ice backing up under your shingles. This product can be installed across the peaks of your roof, along the roof where water flows into the gutters, on both sides of any valley in your roof, and on the sides of walls where the roof connects. If you live where ice is not a concern, talk to your contractor about any benefits of installing this product.

All utilities must be connected to the main house

- Use plenty of vents in the roof and under the eaves so that fresh air can circulate. If moisture is allowed to accumulate in the attic, the plywood could rot and shingles curl up, causing leaks and expensive damage.

- Rafter-truss ties may be required to help hold your roof on during high winds. Refer to the bottom of page 10 for more information and a picture.

Downspouts

- Some cities may not want your downspouts connected to the storm sewer but will require the water to flow into the yard.

Siding

- If at all possible, try to match the siding on your in-law suite to that of the main house. Vinyl siding is attractive and has low maintenance which can save you a lot of work in the future. It helps to hose off the siding with water a couple times a year.

Concrete and Foundation Work

- Check to see whether or not the company supplying the concrete for any sidewalks has a minimum load requirement. This could allow you to have a wider sidewalk or wider steps at no additional cost to you. You may be paying for the concrete anyway. Closely monitor the amount of concrete ordered to get the most for your money.

- A slab foundation is usually less expensive and has less steps. If a crawl space is chosen, the building department will want to know what type of I-beams will be used, their size, number, strength, and placement under the floor. This information can be obtained from your contractor. It's not necessary to have the suite on the same level as the main house, unless required for wheelchair access.

Heating and Air Conditioning

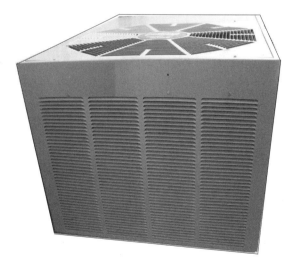

- To people with certain health conditions, air conditioning is essential, because excessive heat can be dangerous to older ones. Also, some allergies may be eased by air conditioning. If you don't want air conditioning at the time of construction, you may want to install the 'A' frame coil with the furnace. Then, at a later time, you can add the compressor unit.

- Gas heat may be preferred by elderly because it feels warm coming out of the registers.

Insulation

- Insulation is very important! Each climate has its own special needs in this regard. Check with your contractor as to what is needed in your area. The cost of natural gas and electricity continue to rise, so it would be wise not to cut corners here! In the attic area, the blow-in kind of insulation seems to do a better job in keeping your home warm in the winter and cool in the summer.

Electrical Outlets

- Communities prefer more electrical outlets to minimize the use of extension cords. This helps in the prevention of fires caused by overloaded circuits.

Cable and Phone Jacks

- Install more outlets for cable television than you think you will need. This is because you may want to rearrange the furniture in your suite. This will keep down the expense of installing more outlets at a later time. Once the drywall is installed, it becomes a more difficult job. The same also applies to telephone jacks. You never know when or where you may need to place your telephone due to changing circumstances.

Windows and Doors

- Your city will want to know the 'U' Value for each window. Ask your contractor for this information. Awning type windows in the bedroom or the den may not be allowed as a safety feature in case of fire. There may be window height requirements in areas where hurricane winds are a problem.

- Building codes often require two exits from your in-law suite. This is for safety reasons. That is why my floor plans show patio doors in the bedroom or other places. You can install a regular door if this is more suitable to your personal needs.

Interior Walls

- Ask your building department where they require fire code drywall installed, and the thickness they require.

- Certain communities may have hallway width requirements as a safety feature.

Final Inspection and Occupancy Permit

- When the final inspection is completed you will receive an occupancy permit at that time. The inspector has no further need to return again.

- The building department may have other requests, too, as each city or suburb has its own requirements. They may even offer suggestions to help you satisfy city codes. Your contractor can help you submit necessary information, or he may do it himself.

- Houses in a development with an association have their own rules that must be followed. It may only concern the type of siding to be used. They will likely want to maintain a uniform look throughout the development.

Take these Twelve Steps to Success:

*If after reading **Build Your Own In-Law Suite** thoroughly, you decide that an in-law suite is practical for your family situation...you may find the following step-by-step directions helpful:*

1. **Have a family discussion.**
   Whose house could this be build onto? Who would pay for the construction? Who will pay for the utility bills and cable?

2. **Determine if a loan is necessary.**
   Check for any low interest rate loans offered by the community or government.

3. **Call the building department or city hall.**
   Ask for their general requirements for this type of addition.
   Is a kitchen allowed? Can you have a private entrance?
   What are property line requirements?

4. **Use the checklist on page 32.**
   Determine the needs of the occupant.

5. **Choose up to three floor plans.**
   Make a copy of the floor plans you choose and take them to the building department to get a verbal okay that any of these plans are workable.

6. **Finalize your choice of floor plan.**
   Note any adjustments.

7. **Locate a reliable contractor.**
   Check with Better Business Bureau.
   Get several bids using the same floor plan.

8. **Decide who will pull the permit.**
   There are pros and cons of pulling your own building permit.
   Read further about this on page 24. The party who pulls the permit legally acts as the contractor.

9. **Review the bids.**
   The builder should give you a cost breakdown for you to consider.
   Negotiate any prices that seem to be too high before signing anything.

10. **Get a signed contract.**
    The builder will draw up a contract with items listed, such as: time of 4 installment payments, date to start construction and complete project, warranty information, and any verbal changes added. Sign only when you are completely happy. Consider having an attorney check the details for you.

11. **If the parent is paying for the suite...**
    Make a signed agreement for the parents peace of mind, concerning the right to continue living in the suite and the compensation of construction cost in the event the property is sold while they're still living. This can help to avoid future misunderstandings. (Optional)

12. **Keep all receipts for any cost of the construction.**
    These may be needed if you sell and capital gains becomes involved.

Suite Finder

Suite	Page	Dimensions	Square Feet	Bdrms	Kitchen	Dining Room	Bath	Laundry Area	Furnace/ Hot Water
1	34	20 x 17	340	1	Wet Bar	-	1	In Bath	-
2	36	20 x 19	380	1	Kitchenette	-	1	In Bath	Optional
3	38	20 x 20	400	1	Standard	-	1	In Bath	-
4	40	22 x 20	440	1	-	-	1	-	-
5	42	22 x 20	440	1	-	-	No	-	-
6	44	20 x 25	500	1	Standard	-	1	Sep. Rm	Yes
7	46	20 x 26	520	1	Wet Bar	Yes	1	-	-
8	48	23 x 23	529	1	Standard	-	1	In Bath	Yes
9	50	23 x 23	529	1	Standard	-	1	In Bath	-
10	52	23 x 24	552	1	Standard	-	1	In Bath	-
11	54	22 x 28	616	1	Standard	Yes	1	In Bath	Yes
12	56	23 x 28	644	1	Standard	-	1	Sep. Rm	Yes
13	58	23 x 28	644	1	Standard	-	1	Sep. Rm	Yes
14	60	22 x 30	660	1	Standard	-	1	Sep. Rm	Yes
15	62	22 x 30	660	1	Standard	-	1	Sep. Rm	Yes
16	64	23 x 30	690	1	Standard	-	1	In Bath	Yes
17	66	26 x 28	728	1	Standard	-	1	Sep. Rm	Yes
18	68	26 x 28	728	1	Standard	Yes	1	In Bath	Yes
19	70	25 x 31	775	1	Standard	Yes	1	In Bath	Yes
20	72	26 x 30	780	1	Eat-In	-	1	In Bath	Yes

Suite Finder

Suite	Page	Dimensions	Square Feet	Bdrms	Kitchen	Dining Room	Bath	Laundry Area	Furnace/ Hot Water
21	74	26 x 30	780	2	Standard	-	1	In Bath	-
22	76	28 x 28	784	1	Eat-In	-	1	In Bath	Yes
23	78	28 x 28	784	1	Eat-In	-	1	Sep. Rm	Yes
24	80	24 x 33	792	2	Standard	-	1	In Bath	Yes
25	82	24 x 34	816	1	Standard	Yes	1	Sep. Rm	Yes
26	84	27 x 31	837	2	Standard	-	1	In Bath	Yes
27	86	24 x 35	840	2	Standard	-	1	Sep. Rm	Yes
28	88	26 x 33	858	1	Standard	Yes	1	In Bath	Yes
29	90	28 x 32	896	2	Standard	-	1	Sep. Rm	Yes
30	92	28 x 32	896	1	Eat-In	-	1	Sep. Rm	Yes
31	94	28 x 32	896	1	Eat-In	-	1	Sep. Rm	Yes
32	96	26 x 35	910	2	Standard	Yes	1	Sep. Rm	Yes
33	98	27 x 34	918	1	Standard	Yes	1	In Bath	Yes
34	100	27 x 34	918	2	Standard	-	1	Sep. Rm	Yes
35	102	28 x 34	952	2	Standard	-	1	Sep. Rm	Yes
36	104	28 x 34	952	2	Standard	-	1½	In Bath	Yes
37	106	28 x 34	952	2	Standard	-	1	In Bath	Yes
38	108	28 x 36	1,008	2	Standard	-	1	In Bath	Yes
39	110	28 x 38	1,064	2	Eat-In	-	1	Sep. Rm	Yes
40	112	28 x 38	1,064	2	Standard	Yes	1½	Sep. Rm	Yes

Checklist

Kitchen
- ❑ Eat-in
- ❑ Mini-kitchen
- ❑ Kitchenette
- ❑ Wet bar
- ❑ Pantry

Cabinets
- ❑ Wood
- ❑ Laminate (Formica)
- ❑ Postform laminate
- ❑ Handles

Countertop
- ❑ Laminate (Formica)
- ❑ Postform laminate
- ❑ Ceramic tile
- ❑ Stone

Appliances
- ❑ Refrigerator side/side
- ❑ Apartment refrigerator
- ❑ Electric range
- ❑ Gas range
- ❑ 2 burner range
- ❑ Dishwasher
- ❑ Apartment dishwasher
- ❑ Microwave ovenhood
- ❑ Exhaust fan

Sink
- ❑ Porcelain
- ❑ Stainless steel
- ❑ Handicap sink
- ❑ Garbage disposal
- ❑ GFI outlets

Rooms
- ❑ Living room w/dining
- ❑ Dining room
- ❑ Den
- ❑ Coat closet
- ❑ Extra half bath

Bathroom
- ❑ Shower stall only
- ❑ Handicapped shower
- ❑ Bathtub w/shower
- ❑ Hand-held shower
- ❑ Whirlpool tub
- ❑ Single or double sink
- ❑ Medicine cabinet
- ❑ Flat mirror
- ❑ Linen closet
- ❑ Extra cabinets
- ❑ Laundry area
- ❑ Exhaust fan
- ❑ Soundproofing
- ❑ Grab bars/reinforce
- ❑ Elongated toilet
- ❑ Elevated toilet
- ❑ Urinal
- ❑ Emergency pull cord
- ❑ GFI outlets

Utility Room
- ❑ Std. washer/dryer
- ❑ Stack washer/dryer
- ❑ Shut-off valve
- ❑ Utility tub
- ❑ Extra cabinets
- ❑ 30 gal. hot water tank
- ❑ 40 gal. hot water tank
- ❑ Gas furnace
- ❑ Electric heat pump
- ❑ Air cleaner
- ❑ Dehumidifier
- ❑ Gas line for dryer
- ❑ 220 line for dryer
- ❑ Electric breaker box

Bedrooms
- ❑ One bedroom
- ❑ Two bedrooms
- ❑ Walk-in closet
- ❑ Ceiling light fixtures
- ❑ Ceiling fans

Doors
- ❑ Private entrance
- ❑ Storm door
- ❑ Door to main house
- ❑ Patio door
- ❑ Pocket doors
- ❑ 36" doors
- ❑ Peephole
- ❑ Deadbolt locks
- ❑ Foyer - linoleum

Windows
- ❑ Awning
- ❑ Double hung
- ❑ Screens
- ❑ Frosted glass

Miscellaneous
- ❑ Linoleum - upgrade
- ❑ Ceramic tile
- ❑ Carpeting - upgrade
- ❑ Wallpaper or borders
- ❑ Painted walls
- ❑ Security system
- ❑ Many electric outlets
- ❑ Plenty of phone jacks
- ❑ Cable TV plugs
- ❑ Insulation - upgrade
- ❑ Fire alarms

Outside
- ❑ Wheelchair ramp
- ❑ Sensor lights
- ❑ Deck
- ❑ Vinyl siding
- ❑ Brick
- ❑ Roof shingles
- ❑ Roof tile
- ❑ Extra vents
- ❑ Water spigot
- ❑ Electrical outlet
- ❑ Hurricane clips
- ❑ Water underlayment

Floor Plans

The following pages contain floor plans for in-law suites, which vary in size from 340 to 1,064 square feet. They are basic and not overly detailed, because everyone's needs and wants are different. Select the basic floor plan you like and have the contractor make size adjustments.

These floor plans are meant to give you ideas in designing an in-law suite that will fit your personal needs. For instance, if the occupant is in a wheelchair, you may need the bathroom and kitchen areas larger for easier maneuvering. The placement and number of doors and windows may need to be changed from what is shown in the floor plans. This is because any number of factors come into play, such as where the in-law suite is attached to the home, the size of the lot, and where the suite will be accessed.

The size of other rooms can be adjusted also. For example, if you don't need an area for a washer and dryer in the bathroom, you could rearrange and adjust the size of the shower, sink, or linen closet.

If you only want a kitchenette instead of a fully equipped kitchen, adjustments can be made. More storage areas or a bar could be added. Your contractor may have other ideas that will better suit your needs.

Keep in mind that all the floor plans can be flipped right to left, front to back, or turned sideways. Your property dimensions may limit the width of the suite you're building.

These suites could also be built up above a garage or another area. The stairway access could come up through the one end of the living room. Other family members might desire to live in the upstairs apartment, while having the elderly parent downstairs. Of course, in-law suites are not limited to just the elderly.

I haven't shown placement of fireplaces in any of the floor plans. The family will want to consider who the occupant will be, and if this would present an added risk of someone catching the house on fire. If the occupant has some type of dementia, it could present a problem. This would also add a considerable amount to the cost of the suite.

It is my sincere hope that the floor plans and ideas in this publication will make your project easier and save you some time and money.

Suite # 1
340 Sq. Ft.

© 1999 Carol J. Klima

1. With this low square footage suite, a separate furnace and water heater may not be needed.

Suite # 1-A
340 Sq. Ft.

20'-0"

10'-0"

7'-0"

17'-0"

PATIO DOOR

CLOSET

CLOSET

WINDOW

BEDROOM
(10' x 10')

**LIVING
ROOM**
(10' x 17')

SHOWER

STACK
WASHER
& DRYER

ENTRANCE

BATHROOM
(10' x 7')

LINEN
CLOSET

CLOSET

APARTMENT
REFRIGERATOR
BELOW
CUPBOARDS
ABOVE

© 1999 Carol J. Klima

**This Plan Suitable
for Converting an
Attached Garage**

Suite # 2
380 Sq. Ft.

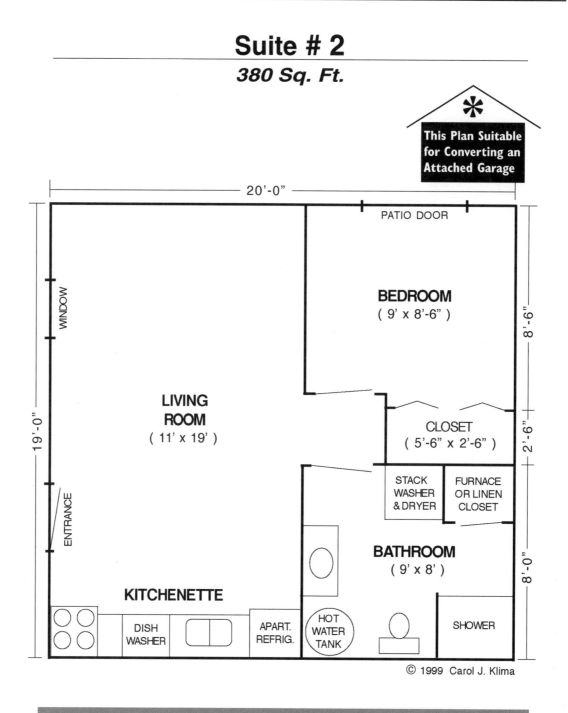

This Plan Suitable for Converting an Attached Garage

20'-0"

PATIO DOOR

BEDROOM
(9' x 8'-6")

8'-6"

WINDOW

LIVING ROOM
(11' x 19')

19'-0"

CLOSET
(5'-6" x 2'-6")

2'-6"

STACK WASHER & DRYER

FURNACE OR LINEN CLOSET

ENTRANCE

BATHROOM
(9' x 8')

8'-0"

KITCHENETTE

DISH WASHER

APART. REFRIG.

HOT WATER TANK

SHOWER

© 1999 Carol J. Klima

2. Kitchen and laundry areas help the parent to keep independence and the low square footage keeps construction cost low.

Suite # 2-A
380 Sq. Ft.

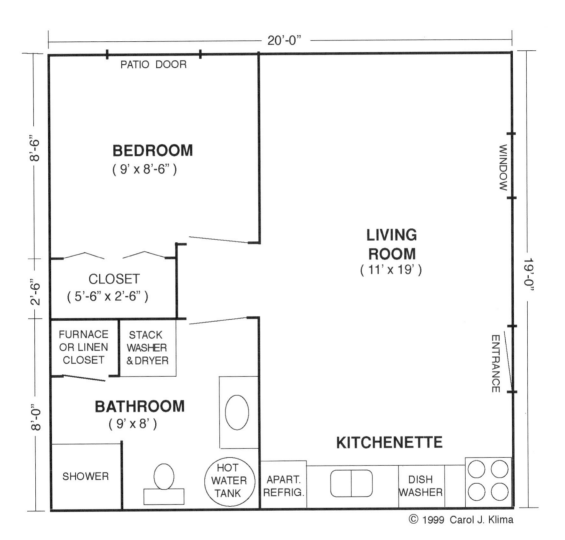

20'-0"

PATIO DOOR

8'-6"

BEDROOM
(9' x 8'-6")

LIVING ROOM
(11' x 19')

WINDOW

19'-0"

2'-6"

CLOSET
(5'-6" x 2'-6")

FURNACE OR LINEN CLOSET

STACK WASHER & DRYER

ENTRANCE

8'-0"

BATHROOM
(9' x 8')

SHOWER

HOT WATER TANK

APART. REFRIG.

KITCHENETTE

DISH WASHER

© 1999 Carol J. Klima

This Plan Suitable for Converting an Attached Garage

Suite # 3
400 Sq. Ft.

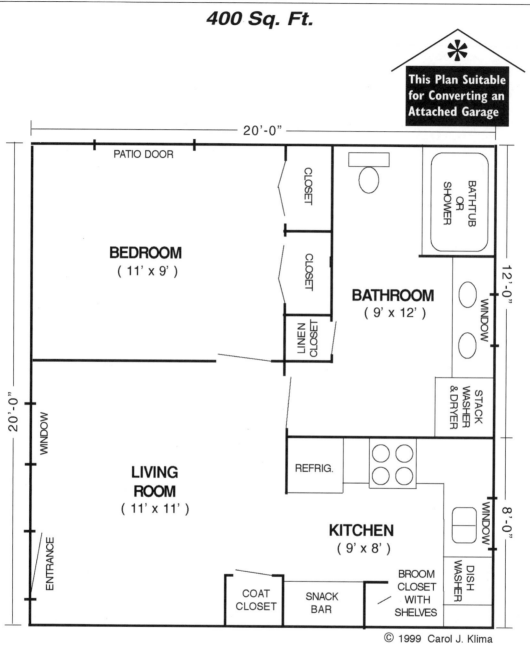

This Plan Suitable for Converting an Attached Garage

3. The entrance door could be changed to the other living room wall to enter directly into the main house. If a furnace is needed, use the extra bedroom closet space with door opening into the bathroom.

Suite # 3-A
400 Sq. Ft.

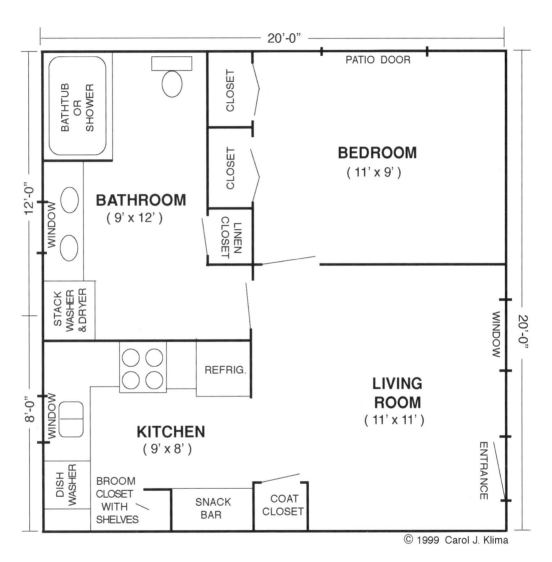

20'-0"

PATIO DOOR

CLOSET

CLOSET

12'-0"

WINDOW

BATHTUB OR SHOWER

BATHROOM
(9' x 12')

BEDROOM
(11' x 9')

LINEN CLOSET

STACK WASHER & DRYER

8'-0"

WINDOW

REFRIG.

LIVING ROOM
(11' x 11')

WINDOW

20'-0"

KITCHEN
(9' x 8')

ENTRANCE

DISH WASHER

BROOM CLOSET WITH SHELVES

SNACK BAR

COAT CLOSET

© 1999 Carol J. Klima

✱ **This Plan Suitable for Converting an Attached Garage**

Suite # 4
440 Sq. Ft.

**This Plan Suitable
for Converting an
Attached Garage**

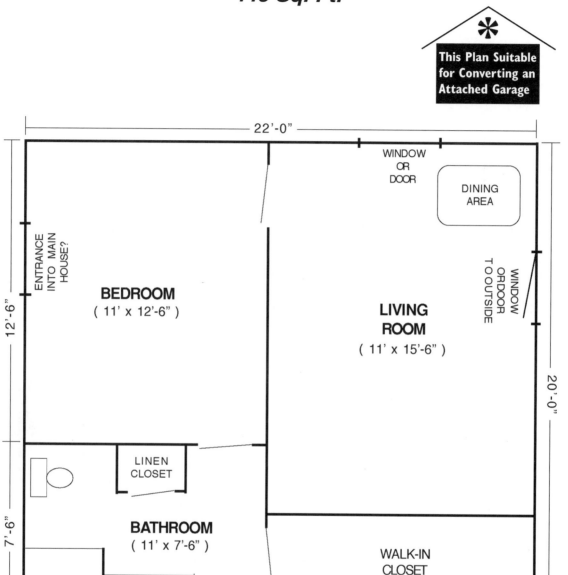

22'-0"

WINDOW
OR
DOOR

DINING
AREA

ENTRANCE
INTO MAIN
HOUSE?

BEDROOM
(11' x 12'-6")

**LIVING
ROOM**
(11' x 15'-6")

WINDOW
OR DOOR
TO OUTSIDE

12'-6"

20'-0"

LINEN
CLOSET

BATHROOM
(11' x 7'-6")

7'-6"

SHOWER

**WALK-IN
CLOSET**
(11' x 4'-6")

4. The door to the main house can be quite adjustable in this layout.
A pocket door between the living room and dining room may be
more convenient.

Suite # 4-A
440 Sq. Ft.

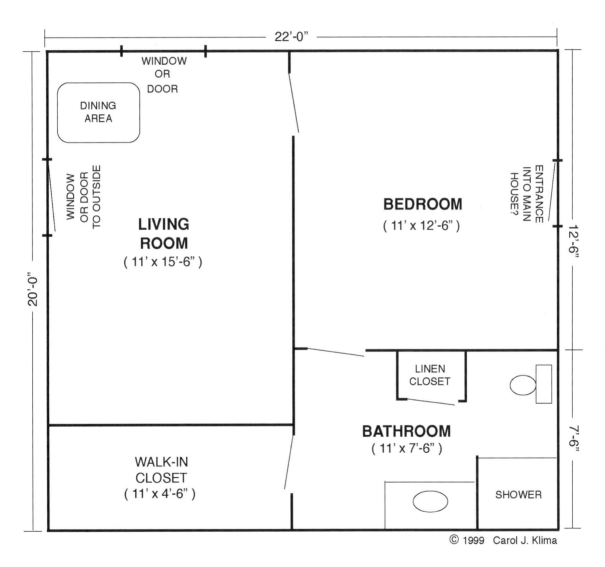

22'-0"

WINDOW
OR
DOOR

DINING
AREA

WINDOW
OR DOOR
TO OUTSIDE

ENTRANCE
INTO MAIN
HOUSE?

BEDROOM
(11' x 12'-6")

LIVING ROOM
(11' x 15'-6")

20'-0"

12'-6"

LINEN
CLOSET

BATHROOM
(11' x 7'-6")

7'-6"

WALK-IN CLOSET
(11' x 4'-6")

SHOWER

© 1999 Carol J. Klima

This Plan Suitable for Converting an Attached Garage

Suite # 5
440 Sq. Ft.

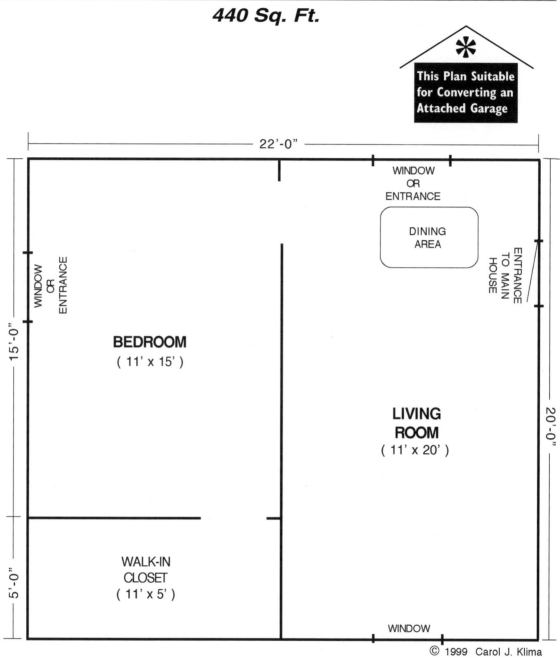

This Plan Suitable for Converting an Attached Garage

22'-0"

WINDOW OR ENTRANCE

DINING AREA

WINDOW OR ENTRANCE

ENTRANCE TO MAIN HOUSE

15'-0"

20'-0"

BEDROOM
(11' x 15')

LIVING ROOM
(11' x 20')

5'-0"

WALK-IN CLOSET
(11' x 5')

WINDOW

© 1999 Carol J. Klima

5. If you're sharing the kitchen and laundry area in the main house, this may be suitable. The large walk-in closet allows plenty of storage. A wet bar or kitchenette could be added to this layout.

Suite # 5-A
440 Sq. Ft.

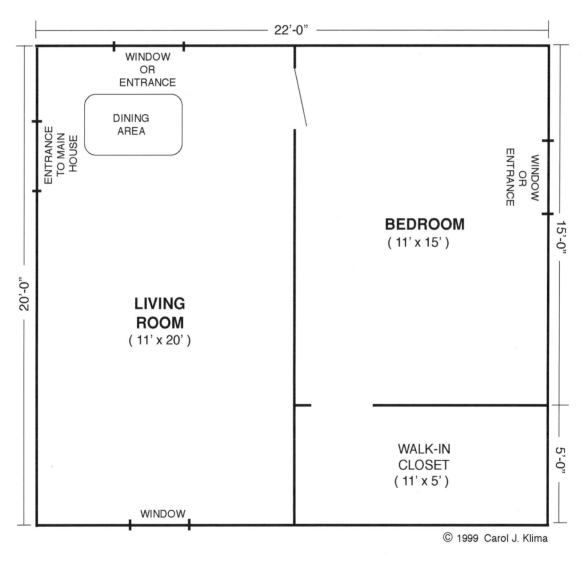

22'-0"

WINDOW
OR
ENTRANCE

DINING
AREA

ENTRANCE
TO MAIN
HOUSE

WINDOW
OR
ENTRANCE

BEDROOM
(11' x 15')

20'-0"

15'-0"

LIVING
ROOM
(11' x 20')

WALK-IN
CLOSET
(11' x 5')

5'-0"

WINDOW

© 1999 Carol J. Klima

**This Plan Suitable
for Converting an
Attached Garage**

Suite # 6
500 Sq. Ft.

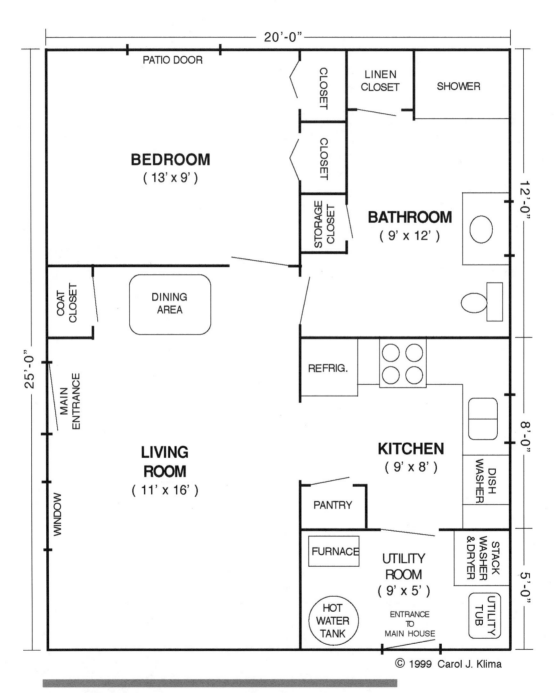

© 1999 Carol J. Klima

6. This is a complete suite with low square footage,
    including a utility tub and a spare storage closet in
    the bathroom.

Suite # 6-A
500 Sq. Ft.

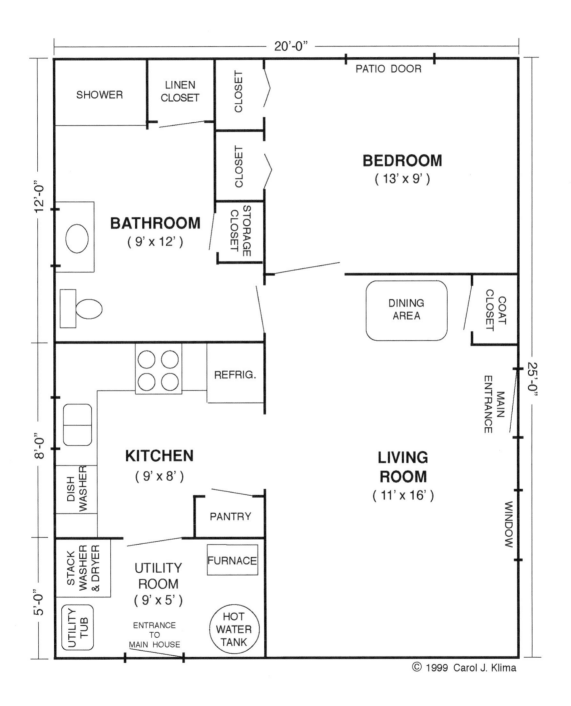

© 1999 Carol J. Klima

Suite # 7
520 Sq. Ft.

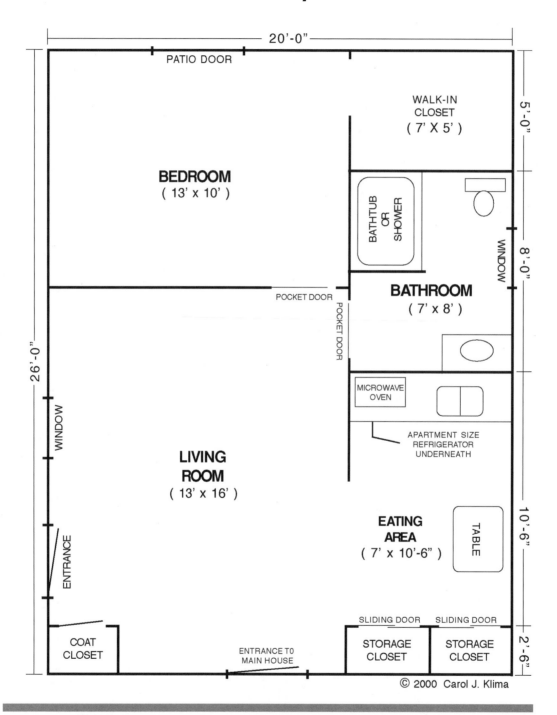

© 2000 Carol J. Klima

7. An open eating area may be easier for a wheelchair occupant to maneuver and pocket doors that slide into the wall are out of the way. This bathroom could easily be rearranged, as also the eating area could be turned into a regular kitchen.

Suite # 7-A
520 Sq. Ft.

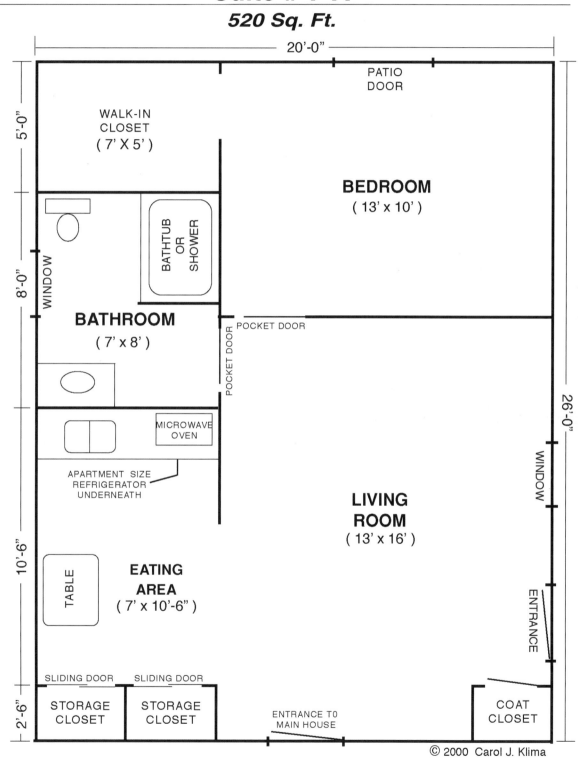

20'-0"

5'-0"

WALK-IN
CLOSET
(7' X 5')

PATIO
DOOR

BEDROOM
(13' x 10')

8'-0"

WINDOW

BATHTUB
OR
SHOWER

BATHROOM
(7' x 8')

POCKET DOOR

POCKET DOOR

26'-0"

MICROWAVE
OVEN

APARTMENT SIZE
REFRIGERATOR
UNDERNEATH

WINDOW

LIVING
ROOM
(13' x 16')

10'-6"

TABLE

EATING
AREA
(7' x 10'-6")

ENTRANCE

2'-6"

SLIDING DOOR　　SLIDING DOOR

STORAGE
CLOSET

STORAGE
CLOSET

ENTRANCE TO
MAIN HOUSE

COAT
CLOSET

© 2000 Carol J. Klima

Suite # 8
529 Sq. Ft.

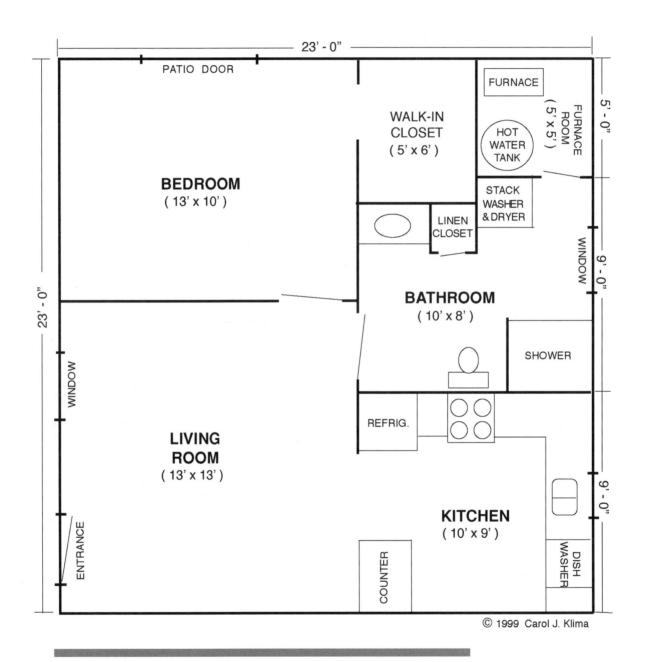

© 1999 Carol J. Klima

8. This is a low square footage suite with everything needed,
    including the furnace and water heater.

Suite # 8-A
529 Sq. Ft.

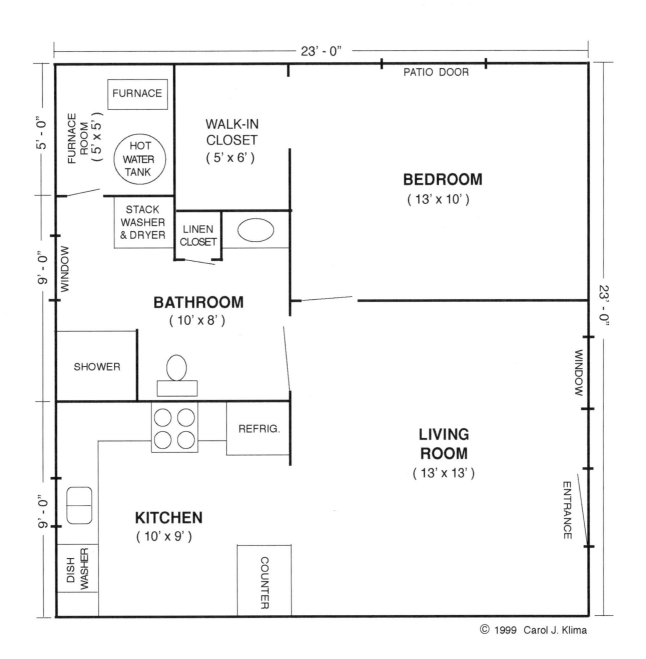

© 1999 Carol J. Klima

Suite # 9
529 Sq. Ft.

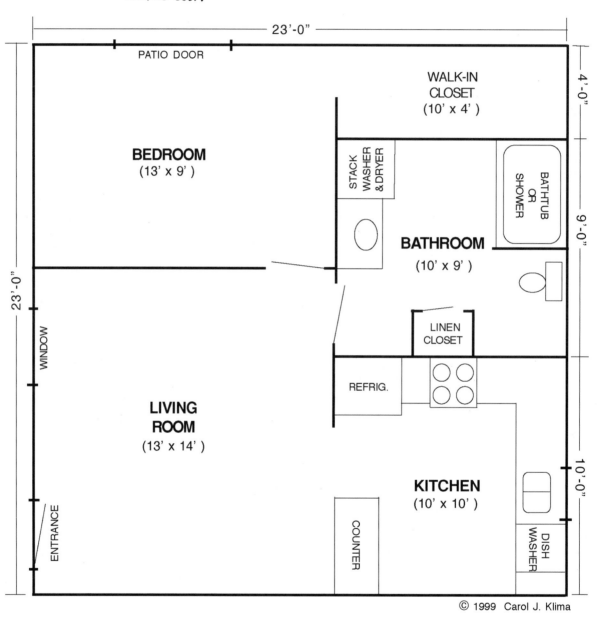

© 1999 Carol J. Klima

9. The bathroom could be rearranged because of its large size.

Suite # 9-A
529 Sq. Ft.

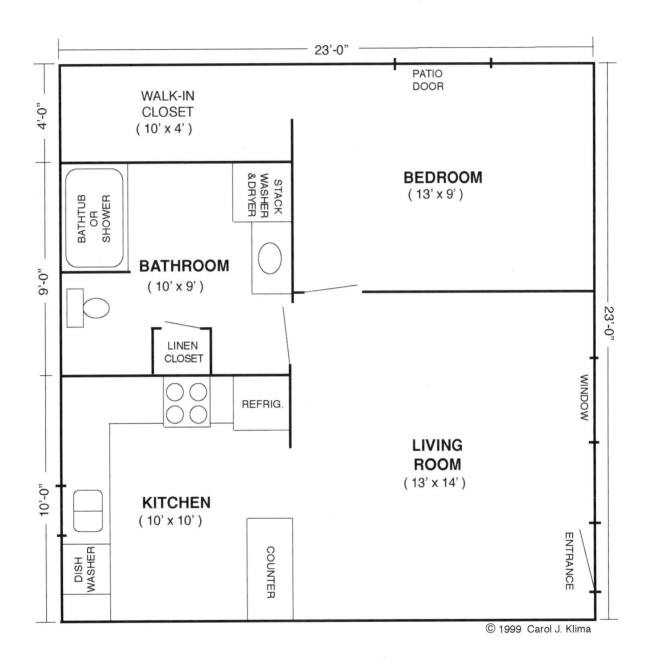

© 1999 Carol J. Klima

Suite # 10
552 Sq. Ft.

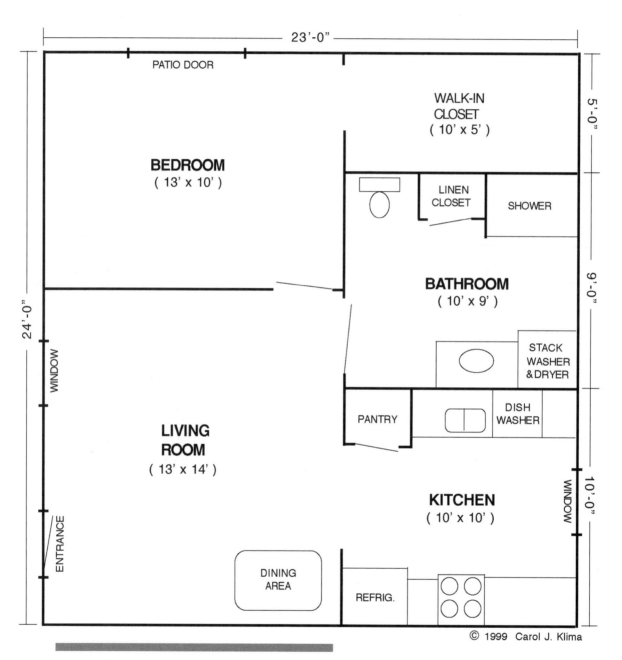

© 1999 Carol J. Klima

10. This is a good suite for a wheelchair
occupant. Pocket doors are advisable.

Suite # 10-A
552 Sq. Ft.

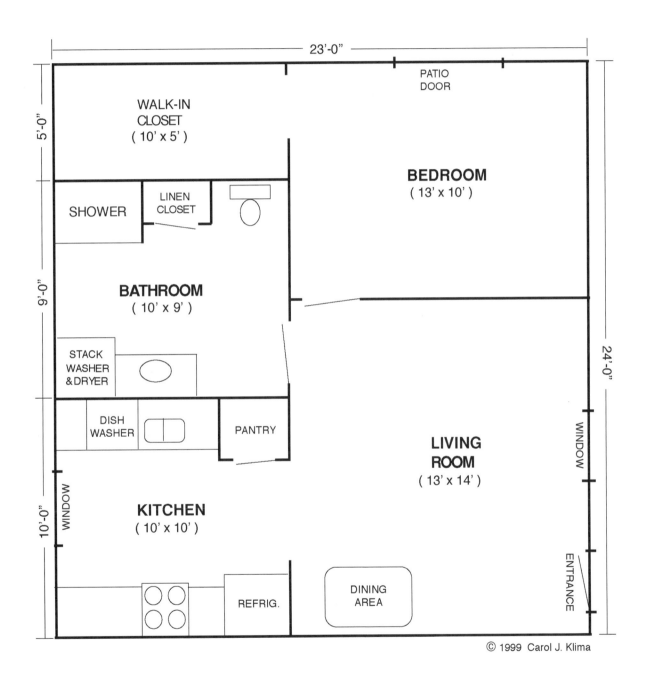

© 1999 Carol J. Klima

Suite # 11
616 Sq. Ft.

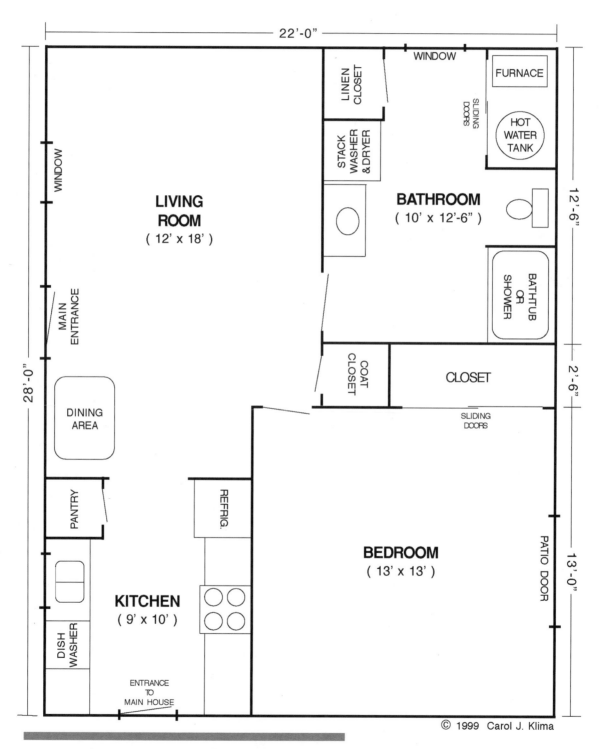

22'-0"

WINDOW

FURNACE

LINEN CLOSET

SLIDING DOORS

HOT WATER TANK

WINDOW

STACK WASHER & DRYER

LIVING ROOM
(12' x 18')

BATHROOM
(10' x 12'-6")

12'-6"

MAIN ENTRANCE

BATHTUB OR SHOWER

COAT CLOSET

CLOSET

2'-6"

28'-0"

DINING AREA

SLIDING DOORS

PANTRY

REFRIG.

BEDROOM
(13' x 13')

PATIO DOOR

13'-0"

DISH WASHER

KITCHEN
(9' x 10')

ENTRANCE TO MAIN HOUSE

© 1999 Carol J. Klima

11. Notice an entrance is at the end of the kitchen.
A desk could be built in next to the refrigerator.

Suite # 11-A
616 Sq. Ft.

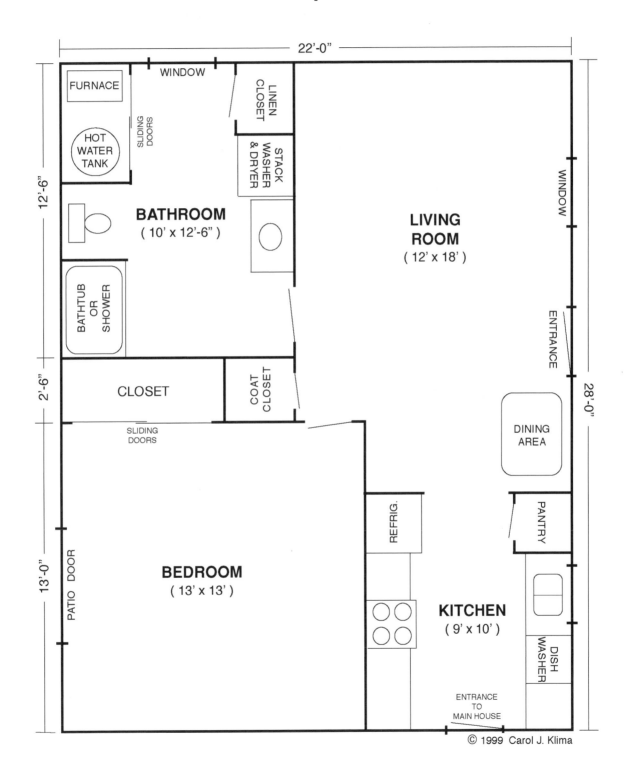

Suite # 12
644 Sq. Ft.

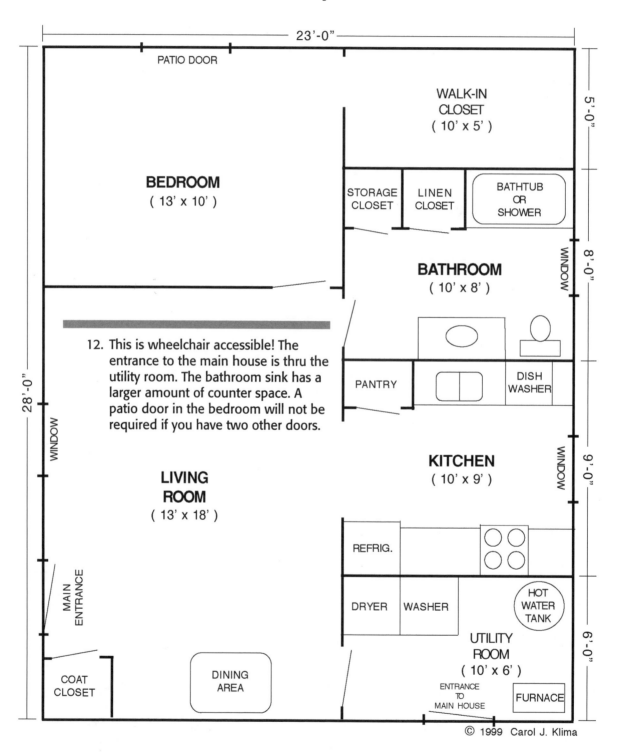

12. This is wheelchair accessible! The entrance to the main house is thru the utility room. The bathroom sink has a larger amount of counter space. A patio door in the bedroom will not be required if you have two other doors.

© 1999 Carol J. Klima

Suite # 12-A
644 Sq. Ft.

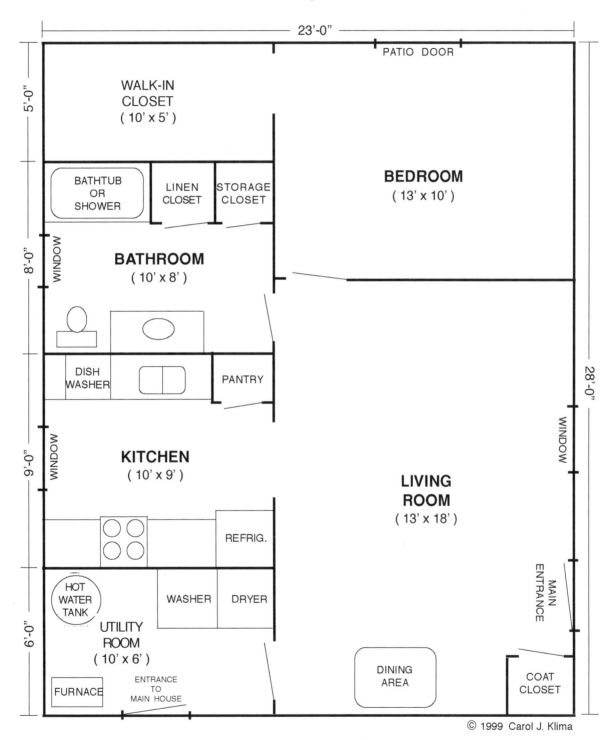

23'-0"

5'-0"

PATIO DOOR

WALK-IN
CLOSET
(10' x 5')

BEDROOM
(13' x 10')

BATHTUB
OR
SHOWER

LINEN
CLOSET

STORAGE
CLOSET

8'-0"

WINDOW

BATHROOM
(10' x 8')

28'-0"

DISH
WASHER

PANTRY

WINDOW

9'-0"

WINDOW

KITCHEN
(10' x 9')

LIVING
ROOM
(13' x 18')

REFRIG.

MAIN
ENTRANCE

6'-0"

HOT
WATER
TANK

WASHER

DRYER

UTILITY
ROOM
(10' x 6')

FURNACE

ENTRANCE
TO
MAIN HOUSE

DINING
AREA

COAT
CLOSET

© 1999 Carol J. Klima

Suite # 13
644 Sq. Ft.

23'-0"

PATIO DOOR

FURNACE

HOT WATER TANK

WALK-IN CLOSET
(5' x 5')

FURNACE ROOM
(5' x 5')

5'-0"

BEDROOM
(13' x 10')

BATHTUB OR SHOWER

LINEN CLOSET

BATHROOM
(10' x 9')

WINDOW

9'-0"

13. A utility room off the kitchen is convenient. This suite is complete but still has lower square footage.

REFRIG.

28'-0"

WINDOW

LIVING ROOM
(13' x 18')

KITCHEN
(10' x 8'-6")

DISH WASHER

8'-6"

MAIN ENTRANCE

PANTRY

WASHER

DRYER

COAT CLOSET

DINING AREA

STORAGE CLOSET

LAUNDRY ROOM
(10' x 5'-6")

UTILITY TUB

ENTRANCE TO MAIN HOUSE

5'-6"

© 1999 Carol J. Klima

Suite # 13-A
644 Sq. Ft.

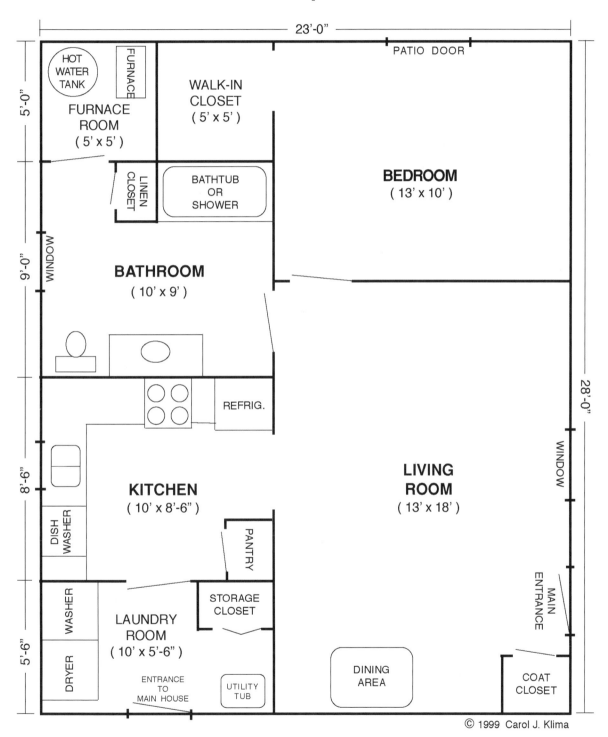

Suite # 14
660 Sq. Ft.

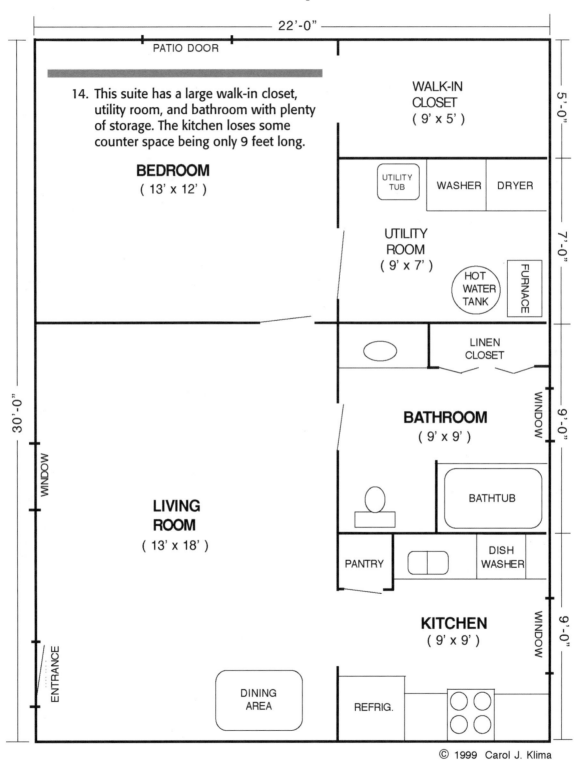

14. This suite has a large walk-in closet, utility room, and bathroom with plenty of storage. The kitchen loses some counter space being only 9 feet long.

22'-0"

PATIO DOOR

WALK-IN CLOSET (9' x 5')

5'-0"

BEDROOM (13' x 12')

UTILITY TUB   WASHER   DRYER

UTILITY ROOM (9' x 7')

HOT WATER TANK   FURNACE

7'-0"

LINEN CLOSET

30'-0"

WINDOW

BATHROOM (9' x 9')

WINDOW

9'-0"

LIVING ROOM (13' x 18')

BATHTUB

PANTRY   DISH WASHER

KITCHEN (9' x 9')

WINDOW

9'-0"

ENTRANCE

DINING AREA   REFRIG.

© 1999 Carol J. Klima

Suite # 14-A
660 Sq. Ft.

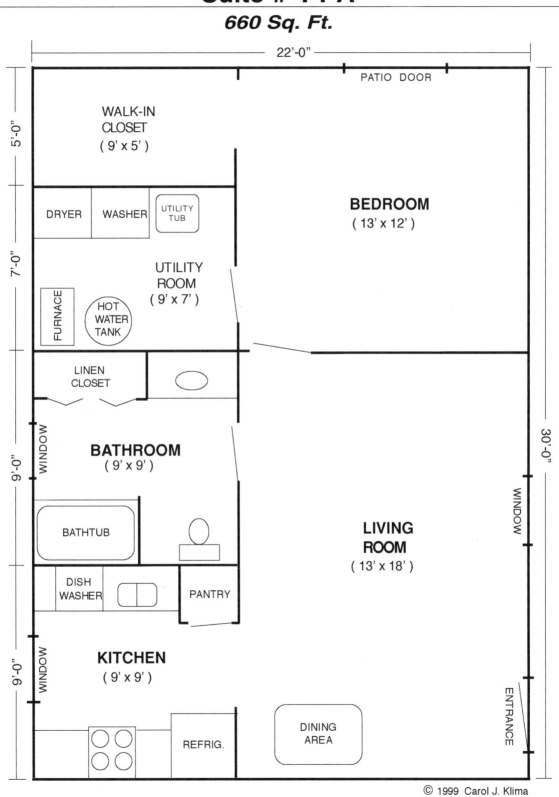

© 1999 Carol J. Klima

Suite # 15
660 Sq. Ft.

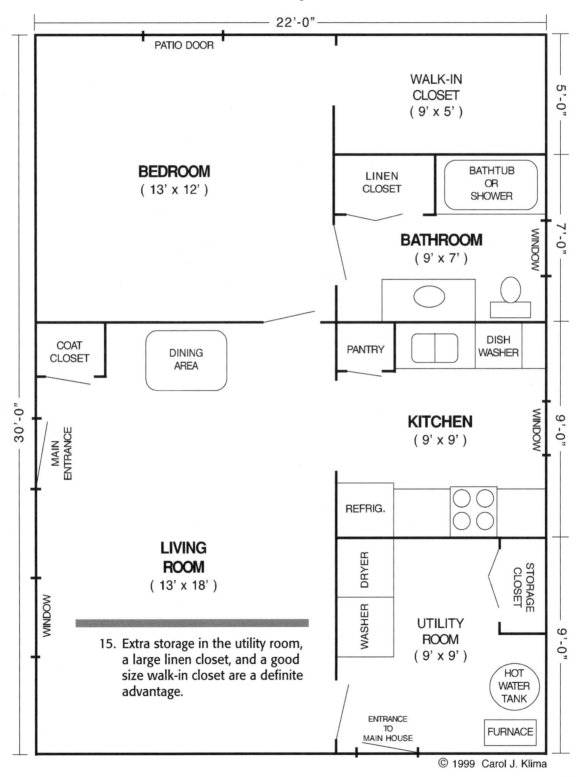

15. Extra storage in the utility room, a large linen closet, and a good size walk-in closet are a definite advantage.

© 1999 Carol J. Klima

Suite # 15-A
660 Sq. Ft.

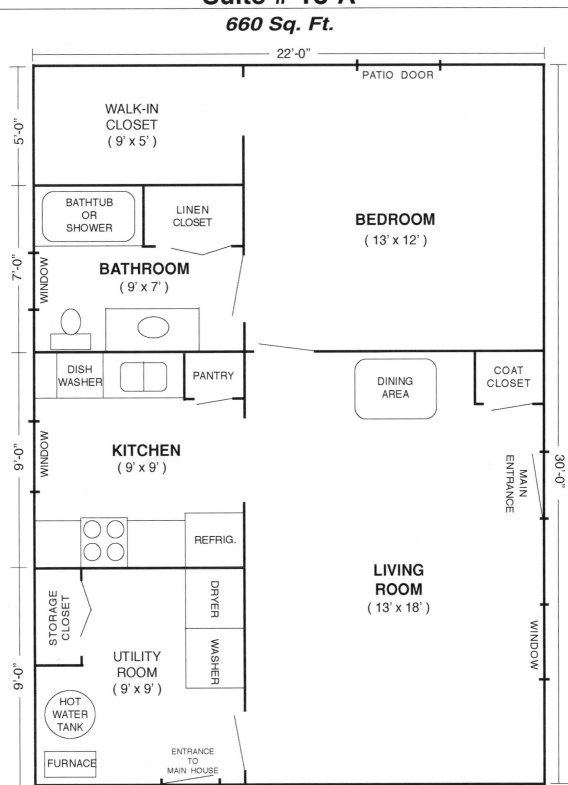

22'-0"

PATIO DOOR

5'-0"

WALK-IN
CLOSET
(9' x 5')

BEDROOM
(13' x 12')

BATHTUB
OR
SHOWER

LINEN
CLOSET

7'-0"

WINDOW

BATHROOM
(9' x 7')

DISH
WASHER

PANTRY

DINING
AREA

COAT
CLOSET

MAIN
ENTRANCE

30'-0"

9'-0"

WINDOW

KITCHEN
(9' x 9')

REFRIG.

DRYER

**LIVING
ROOM**
(13' x 18')

STORAGE
CLOSET

WASHER

WINDOW

9'-0"

**UTILITY
ROOM**
(9' x 9')

HOT
WATER
TANK

FURNACE

ENTRANCE
TO
MAIN HOUSE

© 1999 Carol J. Klima

Suite # 16
690 Sq. Ft.

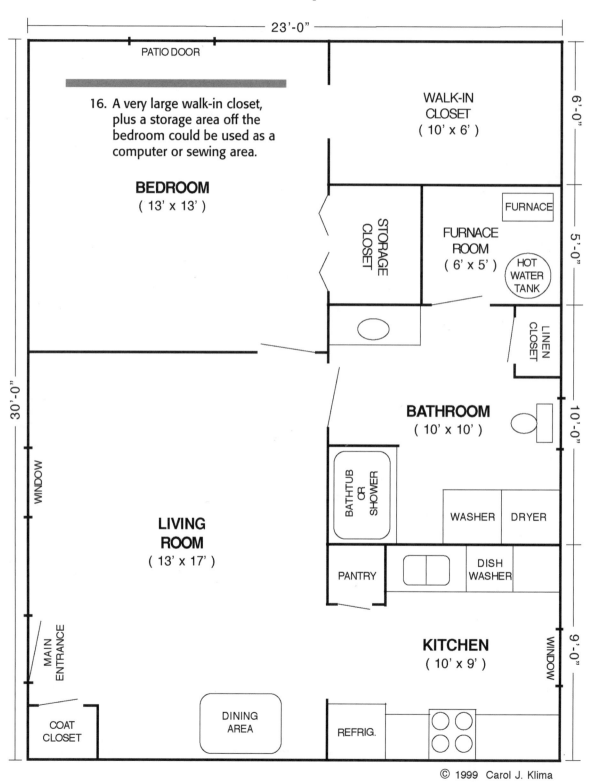

16. A very large walk-in closet, plus a storage area off the bedroom could be used as a computer or sewing area.

PATIO DOOR

WALK-IN CLOSET
(10' x 6')

BEDROOM
(13' x 13')

FURNACE

STORAGE CLOSET

FURNACE ROOM
(6' x 5')

HOT WATER TANK

LINEN CLOSET

BATHROOM
(10' x 10')

WINDOW

LIVING ROOM
(13' x 17')

BATHTUB OR SHOWER

WASHER   DRYER

PANTRY

DISH WASHER

MAIN ENTRANCE

KITCHEN
(10' x 9')

WINDOW

COAT CLOSET

DINING AREA

REFRIG.

23'-0"

30'-0"

6'-0"

5'-0"

10'-0"

9'-0"

© 1999 Carol J. Klima

Suite # 16-A
690 Sq. Ft.

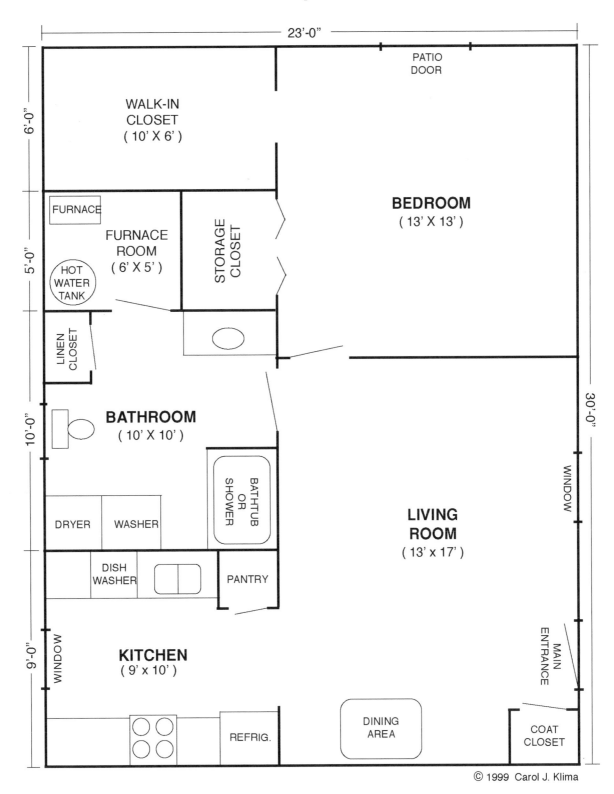

© 1999 Carol J. Klima

Suite # 17
728 Sq. Ft.

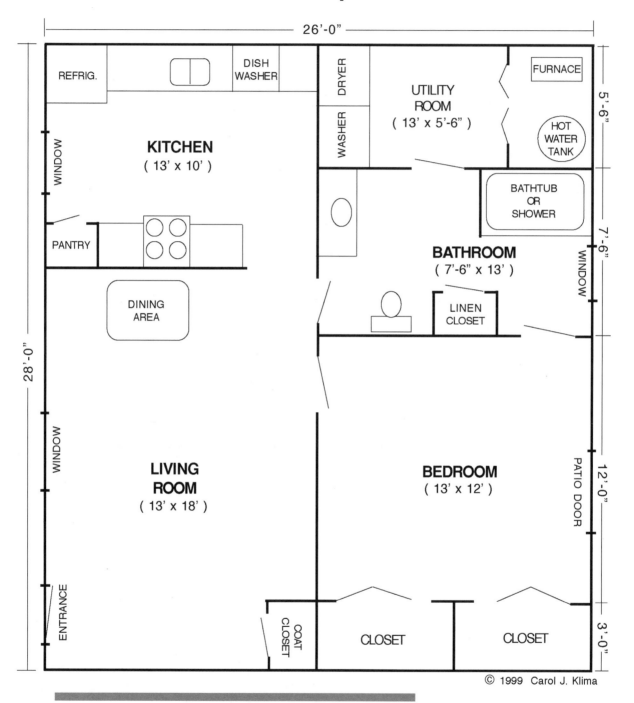

17. Access doors to the main house could go thru the end
    of the living room, the utility room, or the kitchen
    where the window is shown.

Suite # 17-A
728 Sq. Ft.

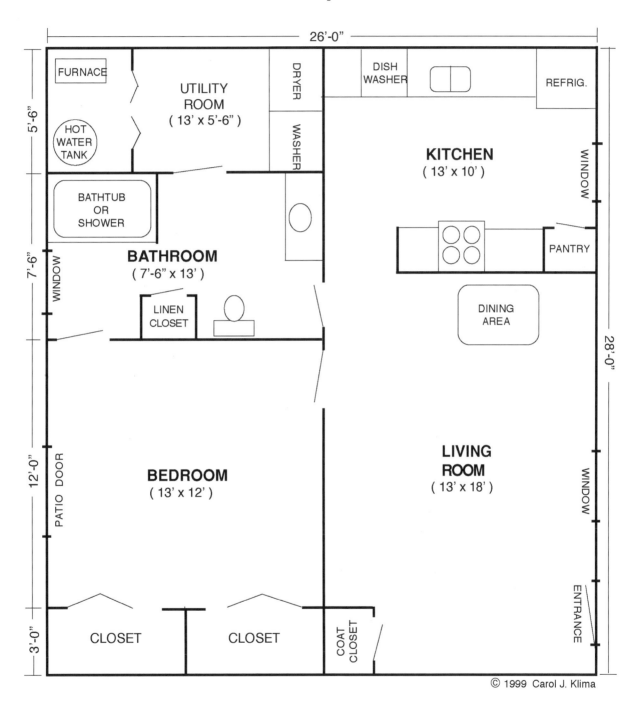

FURNACE

UTILITY ROOM
(13' x 5'-6")

DRYER

WASHER

DISH WASHER

REFRIG.

5'-6"

HOT WATER TANK

KITCHEN
(13' x 10')

WINDOW

BATHTUB OR SHOWER

PANTRY

BATHROOM
(7'-6" x 13')

7'-6"

WINDOW

LINEN CLOSET

DINING AREA

28'-0"

12'-0"

PATIO DOOR

BEDROOM
(13' x 12')

LIVING ROOM
(13' x 18')

WINDOW

ENTRANCE

3'-0"

CLOSET

CLOSET

COAT CLOSET

26'-0"

© 1999 Carol J. Klima

Suite # 18
728 Sq. Ft.

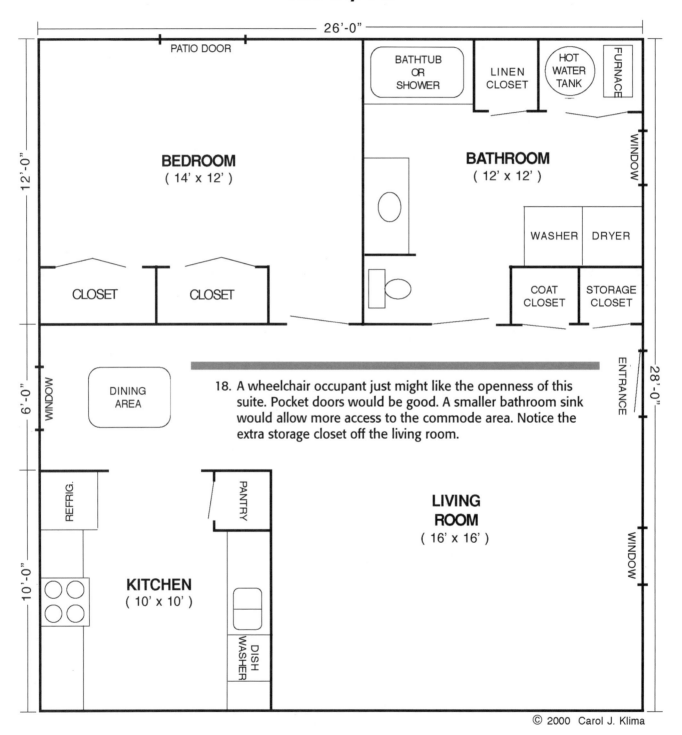

26'-0"

PATIO DOOR

BATHTUB OR SHOWER

LINEN CLOSET

HOT WATER TANK

FURNACE

12'-0"

BEDROOM
(14' x 12')

BATHROOM
(12' x 12')

WINDOW

WASHER | DRYER

CLOSET

CLOSET

COAT CLOSET

STORAGE CLOSET

6'-0"

WINDOW

DINING AREA

ENTRANCE

28'-0"

18. A wheelchair occupant just might like the openness of this suite. Pocket doors would be good. A smaller bathroom sink would allow more access to the commode area. Notice the extra storage closet off the living room.

REFRIG.

PANTRY

LIVING ROOM
(16' x 16')

WINDOW

10'-0"

KITCHEN
(10' x 10')

DISH WASHER

© 2000 Carol J. Klima

Suite # 18-A
728 Sq. Ft.

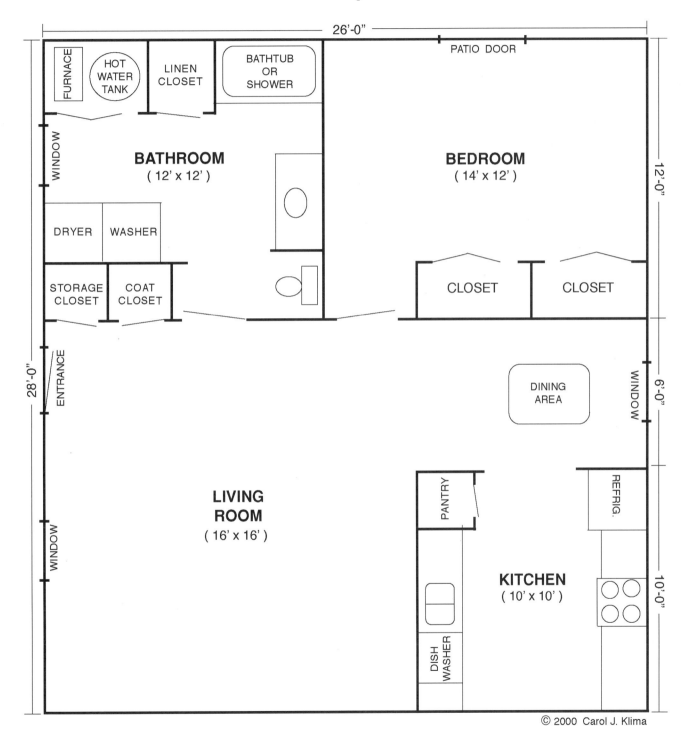

© 2000 Carol J. Klima

Suite # 19
775 Sq. Ft.

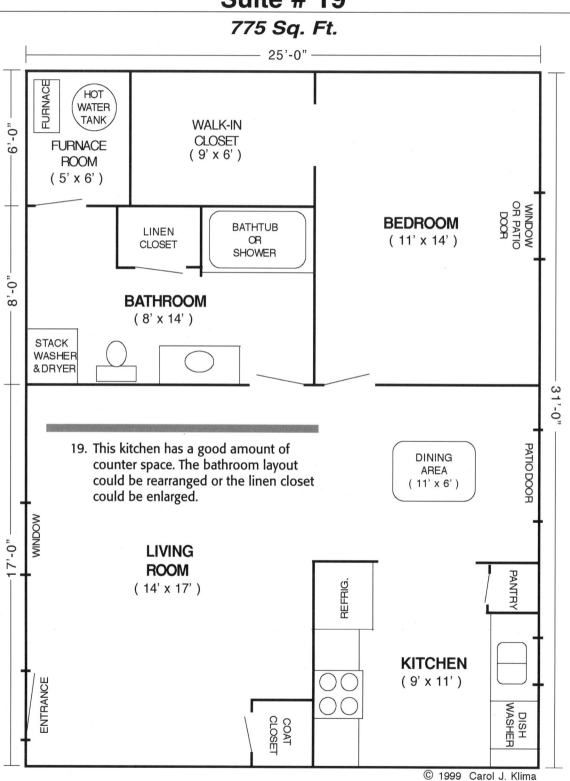

19. This kitchen has a good amount of counter space. The bathroom layout could be rearranged or the linen closet could be enlarged.

© 1999 Carol J. Klima

Suite # 19-A
775 Sq. Ft.

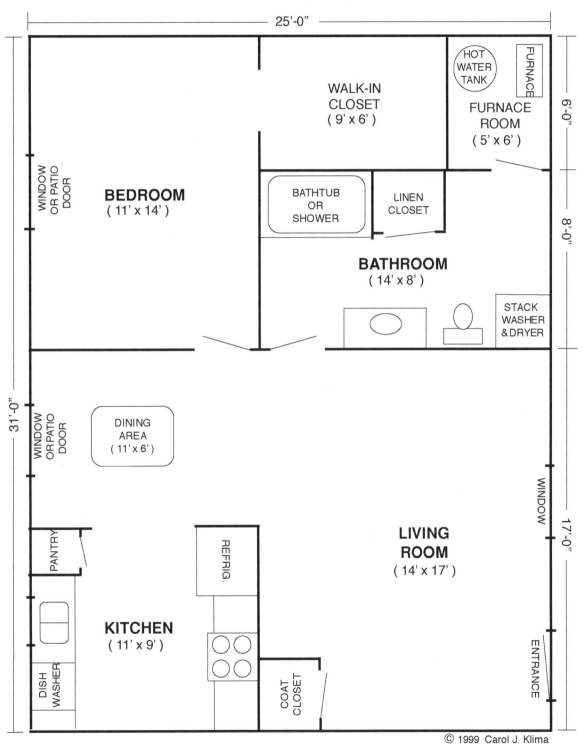

WALK-IN
CLOSET
(9' x 6')

HOT
WATER
TANK

FURNACE

FURNACE
ROOM
(5' x 6')

6'-0"

WINDOW
OR PATIO
DOOR

BEDROOM
(11' x 14')

BATHTUB
OR
SHOWER

LINEN
CLOSET

BATHROOM
(14' x 8')

8'-0"

STACK
WASHER
& DRYER

25'-0"

31'-0"

WINDOW
OR PATIO
DOOR

DINING
AREA
(11' x 6')

LIVING
ROOM
(14' x 17')

WINDOW

17'-0"

PANTRY

REFRIG.

KITCHEN
(11' x 9')

DISH
WASHER

COAT
CLOSET

ENTRANCE

© 1999 Carol J. Klima

Suite # 20
780 Sq. Ft.

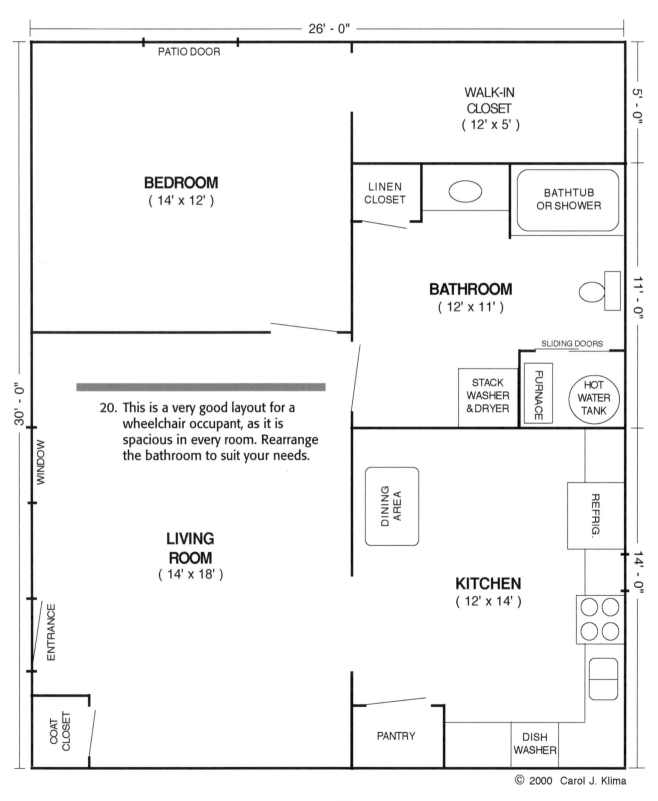

20. This is a very good layout for a wheelchair occupant, as it is spacious in every room. Rearrange the bathroom to suit your needs.

Suite # 20-A
780 Sq. Ft.

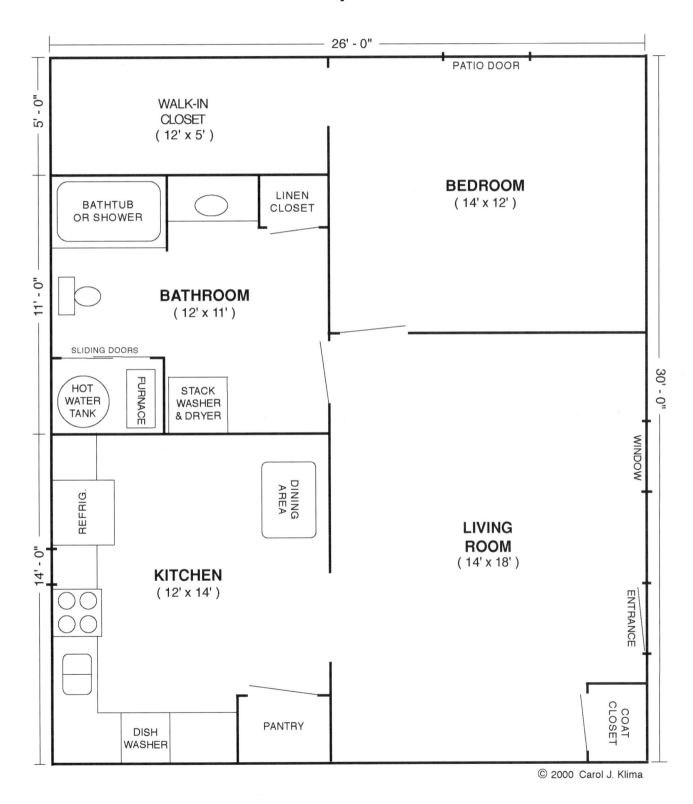

Suite # 21
780 Sq. Ft.

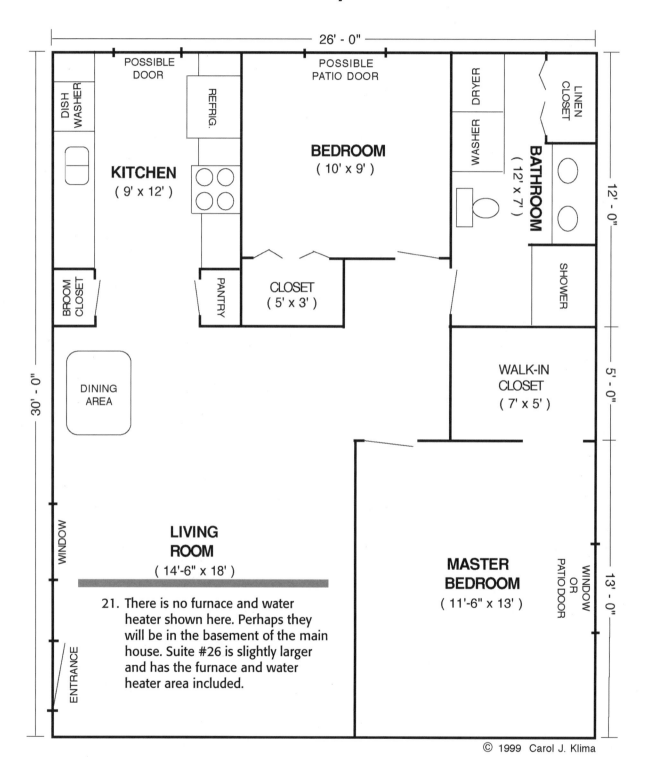

21. There is no furnace and water heater shown here. Perhaps they will be in the basement of the main house. Suite #26 is slightly larger and has the furnace and water heater area included.

© 1999 Carol J. Klima

Suite # 21-A
780 Sq. Ft.

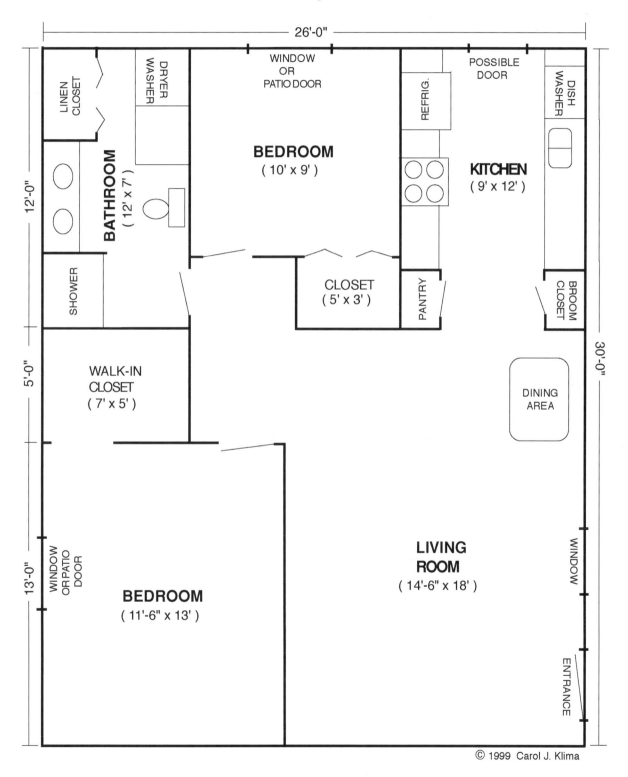

LINEN CLOSET

WASHER DRYER

WINDOW OR PATIO DOOR

REFRIG.

POSSIBLE DOOR

DISH WASHER

26'-0"

12'-0"

BEDROOM
(10' x 9')

KITCHEN
(9' x 12')

BATHROOM
(12' x 7')

SHOWER

CLOSET
(5' x 3')

PANTRY

BROOM CLOSET

30'-0"

5'-0"

WALK-IN CLOSET
(7' x 5')

DINING AREA

13'-0"

WINDOW OR PATIO DOOR

BEDROOM
(11'-6" x 13')

LIVING ROOM
(14'-6" x 18')

WINDOW

ENTRANCE

Suite # 22
784 Sq. Ft.

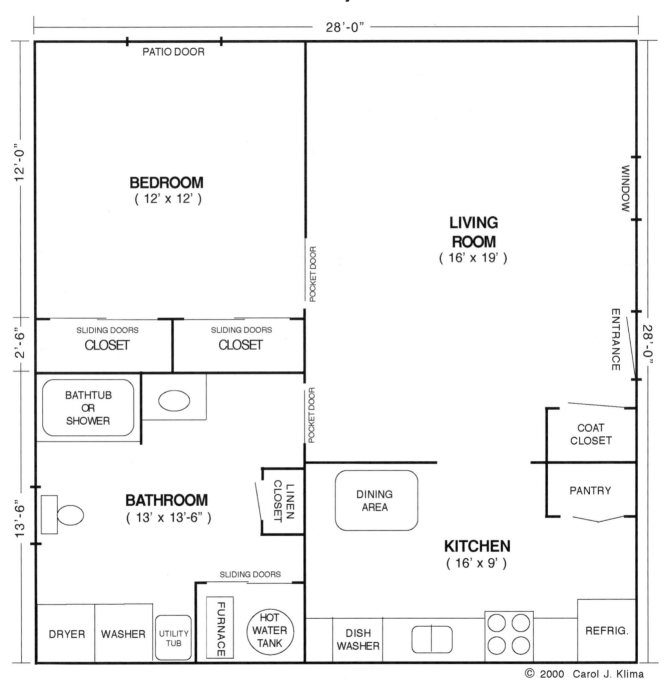

© 2000 Carol J. Klima

22. This suite is very good for one in a wheelchair. The kitchen pantry could be
    left as open shelving with no door.

Suite # 22-A
784 Sq. Ft.

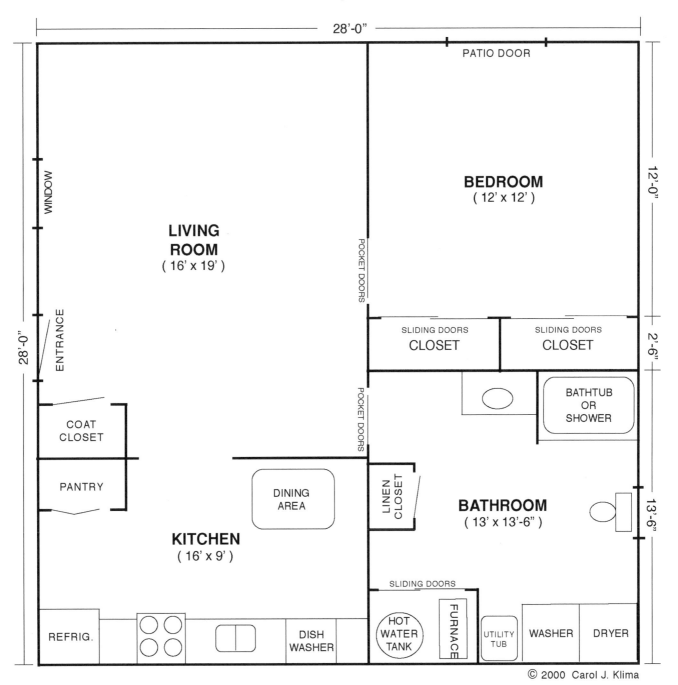

© 2000 Carol J. Klima

Suite # 23
784 Sq. Ft.

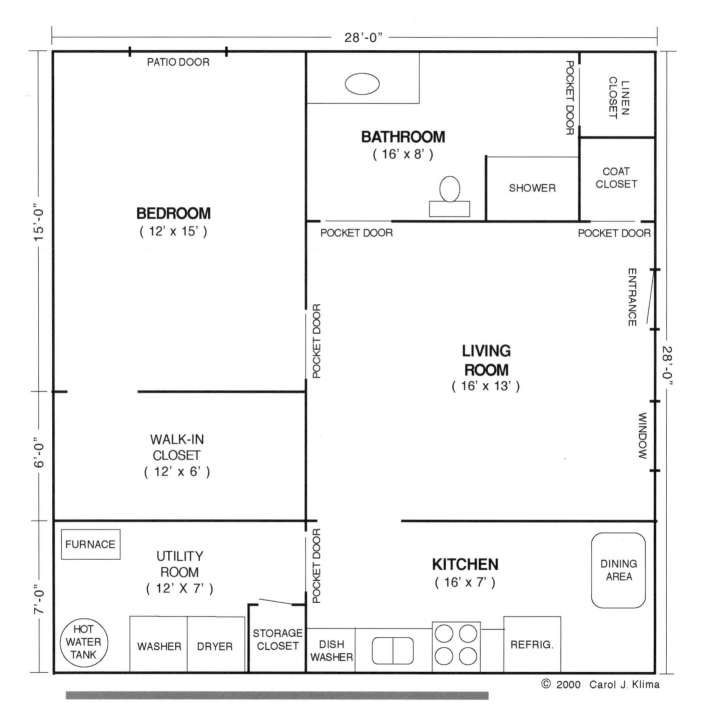

© 2000 Carol J. Klima

23. A door from the main house could come thru the kitchen. The utility room could be rearranged for an entrance door to the main house. Notice the large walk-in closet.

Suite # 23-A
784 Sq. Ft.

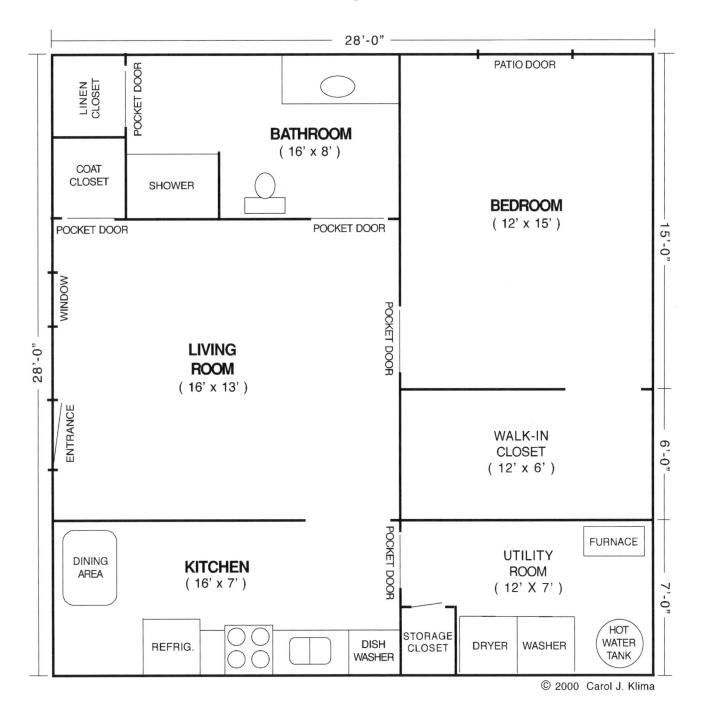

28'-0"

LINEN CLOSET

POCKET DOOR

PATIO DOOR

COAT CLOSET

SHOWER

BATHROOM
(16' x 8')

BEDROOM
(12' x 15')

15'-0"

POCKET DOOR   POCKET DOOR

WINDOW

POCKET DOOR

28'-0"

LIVING ROOM
(16' x 13')

ENTRANCE

WALK-IN CLOSET
(12' x 6')

6'-0"

POCKET DOOR

FURNACE

DINING AREA

KITCHEN
(16' x 7')

UTILITY ROOM
(12' X 7')

7'-0"

REFRIG.

DISH WASHER

STORAGE CLOSET

DRYER   WASHER

HOT WATER TANK

© 2000 Carol J. Klima

Suite # 24
792 Sq. Ft.

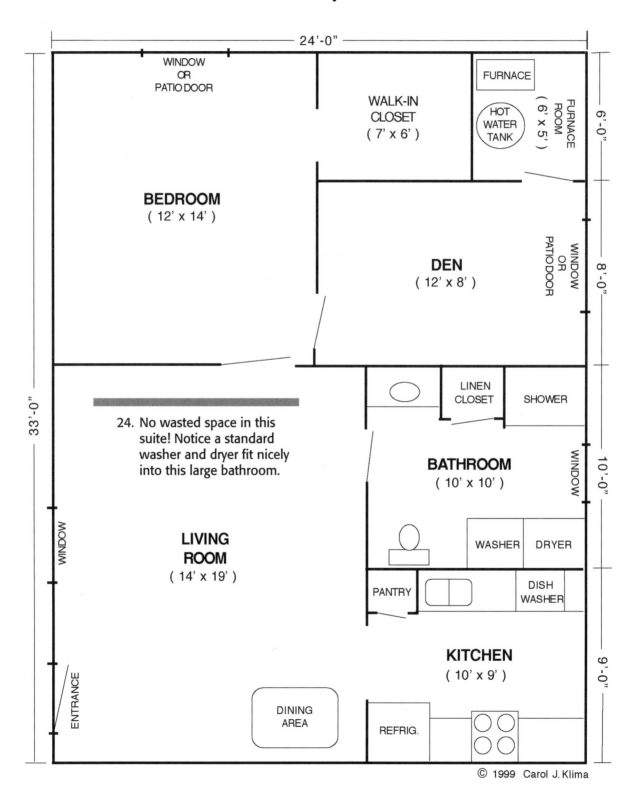

24. No wasted space in this suite! Notice a standard washer and dryer fit nicely into this large bathroom.

© 1999 Carol J. Klima

Suite # 24-A
792 Sq. Ft.

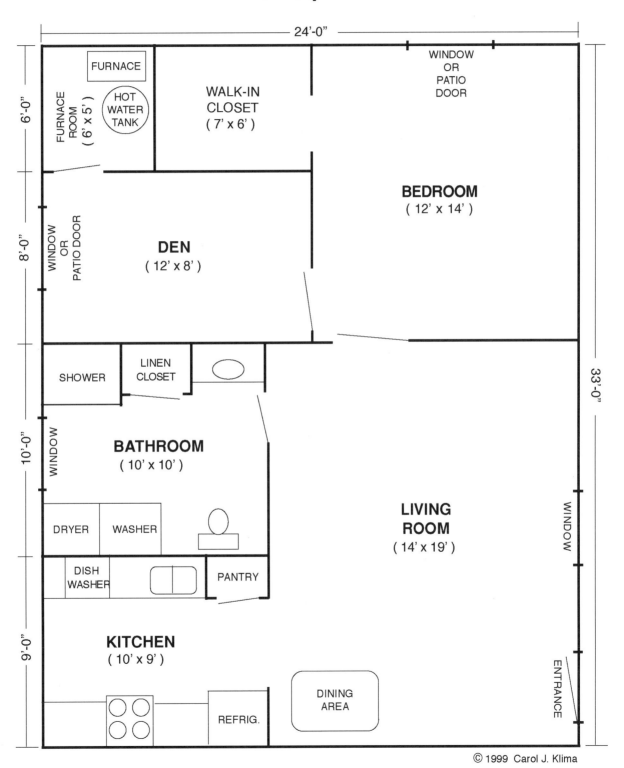

Suite # 25
816 Sq. Ft.

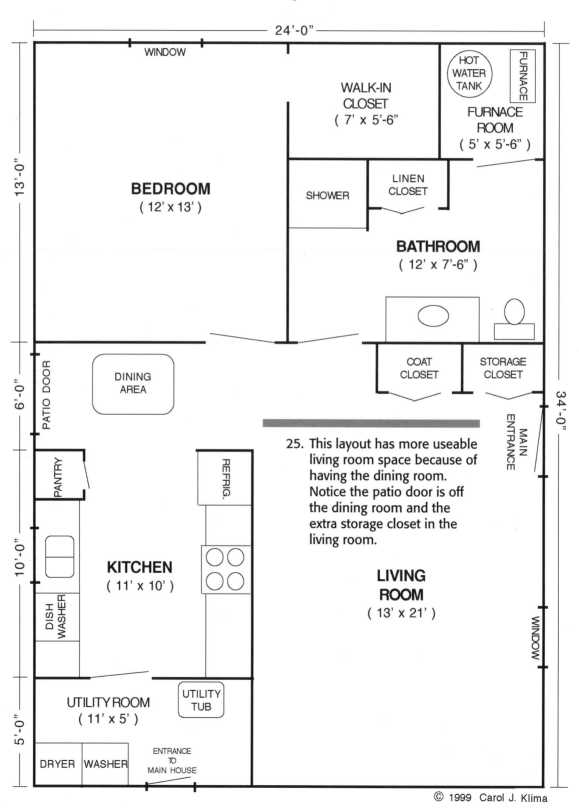

25. This layout has more useable living room space because of having the dining room. Notice the patio door is off the dining room and the extra storage closet in the living room.

© 1999 Carol J. Klima

Suite # 25-A
816 Sq. Ft.

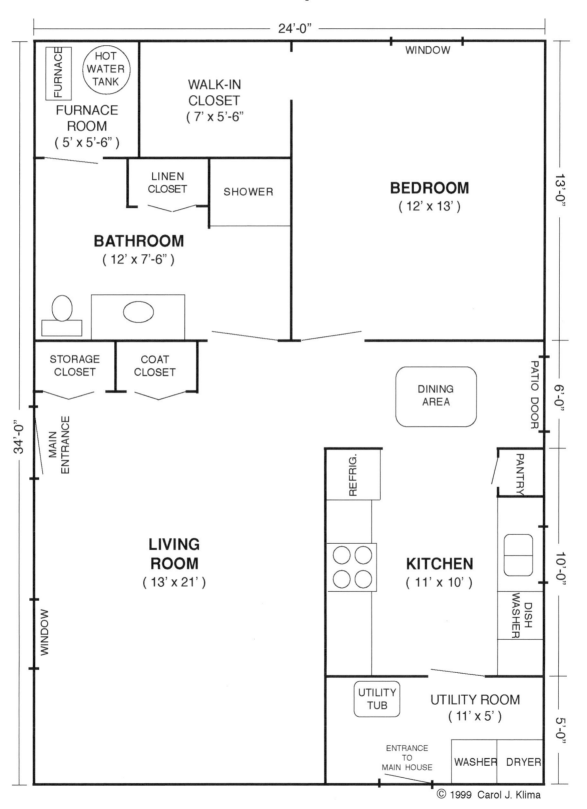

Suite # 26
837 Sq. Ft.

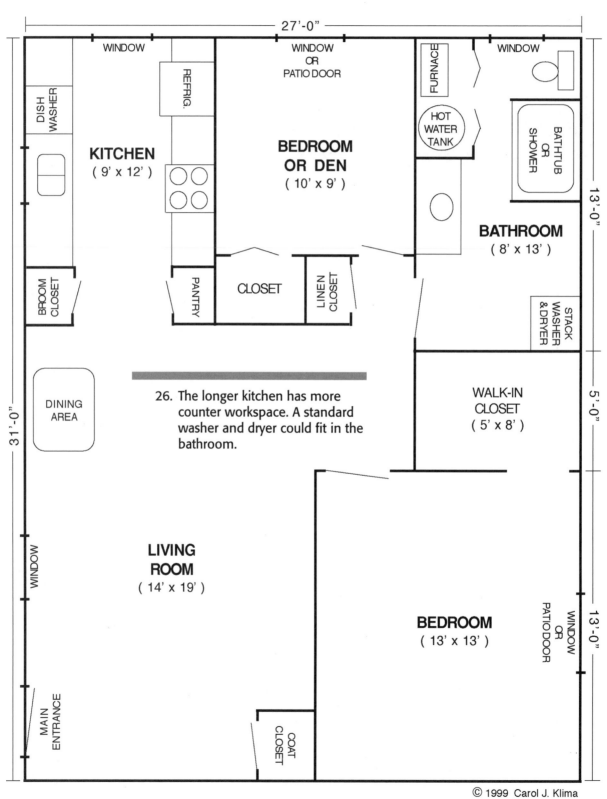

26. The longer kitchen has more counter workspace. A standard washer and dryer could fit in the bathroom.

Suite # 26-A
837 Sq. Ft.

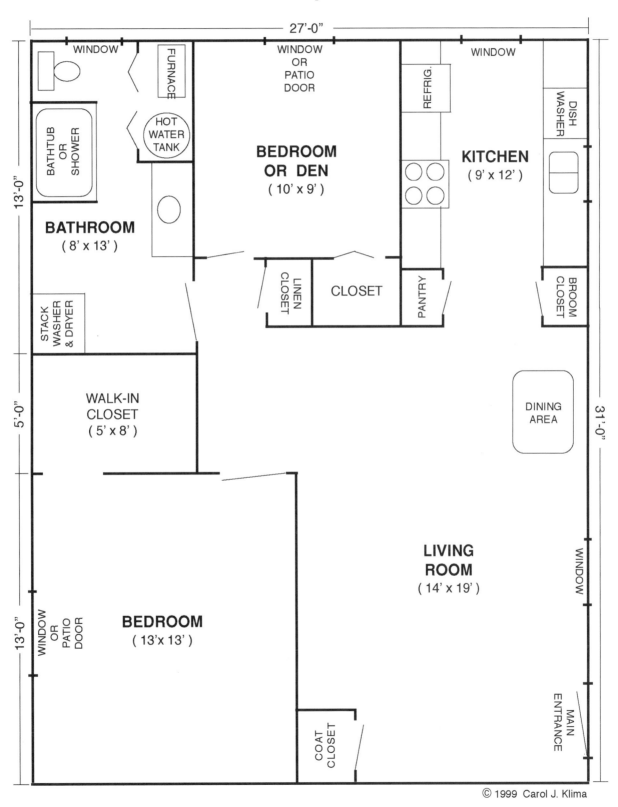

© 1999 Carol J. Klima

Suite # 27
840 Sq. Ft.

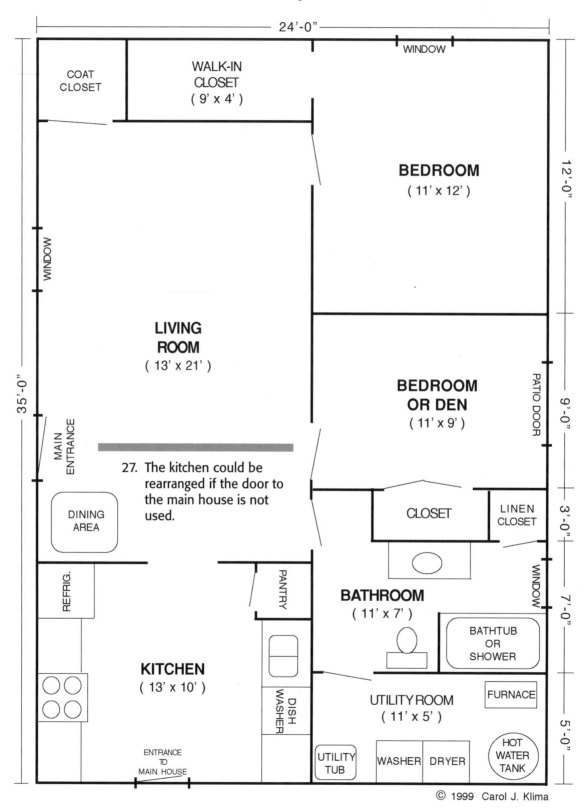

27. The kitchen could be rearranged if the door to the main house is not used.

© 1999 Carol J. Klima

Suite # 27-A
840 Sq. Ft.

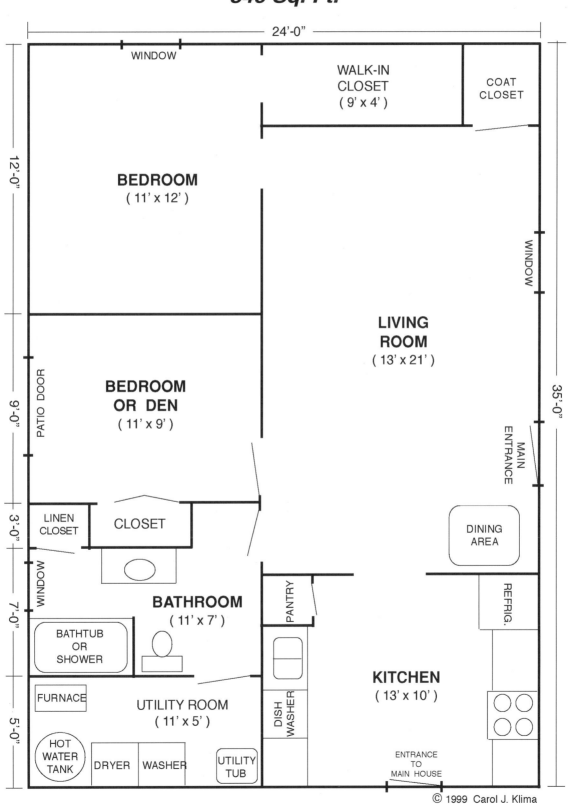

WINDOW

WALK-IN
CLOSET
(9' x 4')

COAT
CLOSET

24'-0"

12'-0"

BEDROOM
(11' x 12')

**LIVING
ROOM**
(13' x 21')

WINDOW

PATIO DOR

9'-0"

**BEDROOM
OR DEN**
(11' x 9')

35'-0"

MAIN
ENTRANCE

LINEN
CLOSET

CLOSET

DINING
AREA

3'-0"

WINDOW

REFRIG.

7'-0"

BATHROOM
(11' x 7')

PANTRY

KITCHEN
(13' x 10')

BATHTUB
OR
SHOWER

FURNACE

UTILITY ROOM
(11' x 5')

DISH
WASHER

5'-0"

HOT
WATER
TANK

DRYER   WASHER

UTILITY
TUB

ENTRANCE
TO
MAIN HOUSE

© 1999 Carol J. Klima

Suite # 28
858 Sq. Ft.

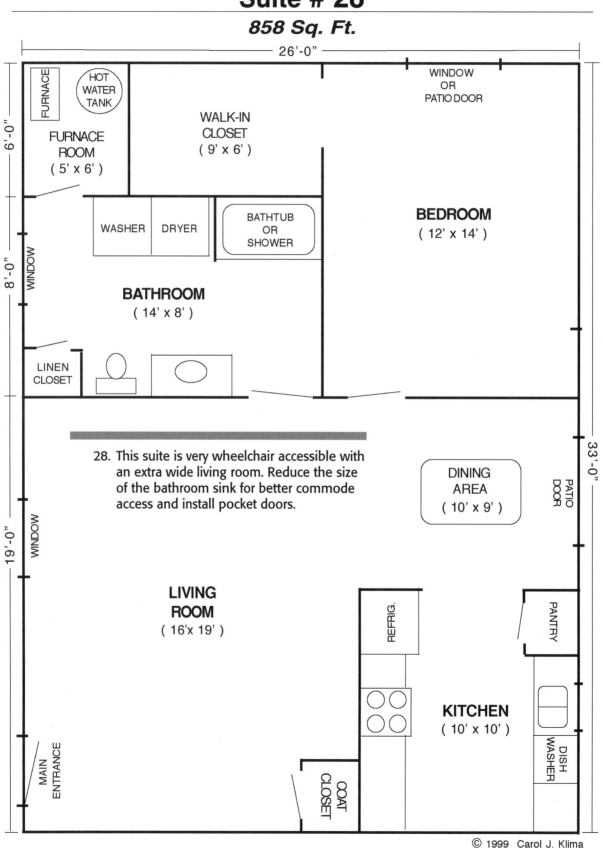

28'-0"

6'-0"

8'-0"

19'-0"

33'-0"

FURNACE

HOT
WATER
TANK

FURNACE
ROOM
(5' x 6')

WALK-IN
CLOSET
(9' x 6')

WINDOW
OR
PATIO DOOR

BEDROOM
(12' x 14')

WASHER | DRYER

BATHTUB
OR
SHOWER

WINDOW

BATHROOM
(14' x 8')

LINEN
CLOSET

28. This suite is very wheelchair accessible with an extra wide living room. Reduce the size of the bathroom sink for better commode access and install pocket doors.

DINING
AREA
(10' x 9')

PATIO DOOR

WINDOW

LIVING
ROOM
(16'x 19')

REFRIG.

PANTRY

KITCHEN
(10' x 10')

MAIN ENTRANCE

COAT
CLOSET

DISH
WASHER

Suite # 28-A
858 Sq. Ft.

© 1999 Carol J. Klima

Suite # 29
896 Sq. Ft.

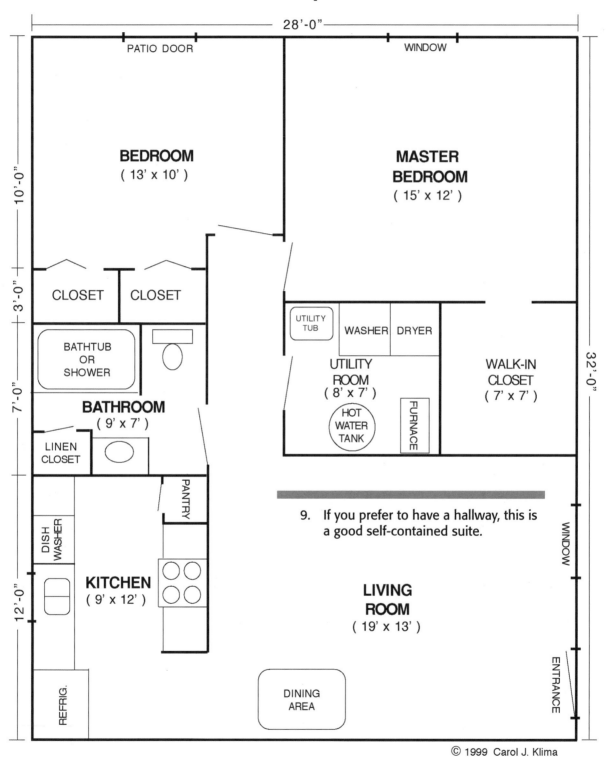

9. If you prefer to have a hallway, this is a good self-contained suite.

© 1999 Carol J. Klima

Suite # 29-A
896 Sq. Ft.

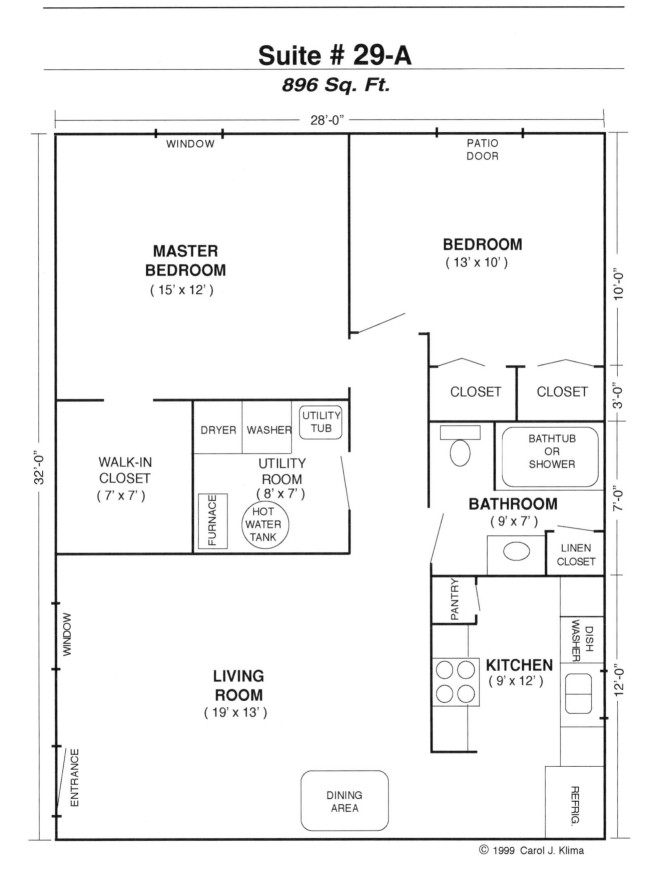

MASTER
BEDROOM
(15' x 12')

WINDOW

PATIO
DOOR

BEDROOM
(13' x 10')

28'-0"

32'-0"

10'-0"

WALK-IN
CLOSET
(7' x 7')

DRYER WASHER

UTILITY
TUB

UTILITY
ROOM
(8' x 7')

FURNACE

HOT
WATER
TANK

CLOSET

CLOSET

3'-0"

BATHTUB
OR
SHOWER

7'-0"

BATHROOM
(9' x 7')

LINEN
CLOSET

WINDOW

LIVING
ROOM
(19' x 13')

PANTRY

KITCHEN
(9' x 12')

DISH
WASHER

12'-0"

ENTRANCE

DINING
AREA

REFRIG.

© 1999 Carol J. Klima

Suite # 30
896 Sq. Ft.

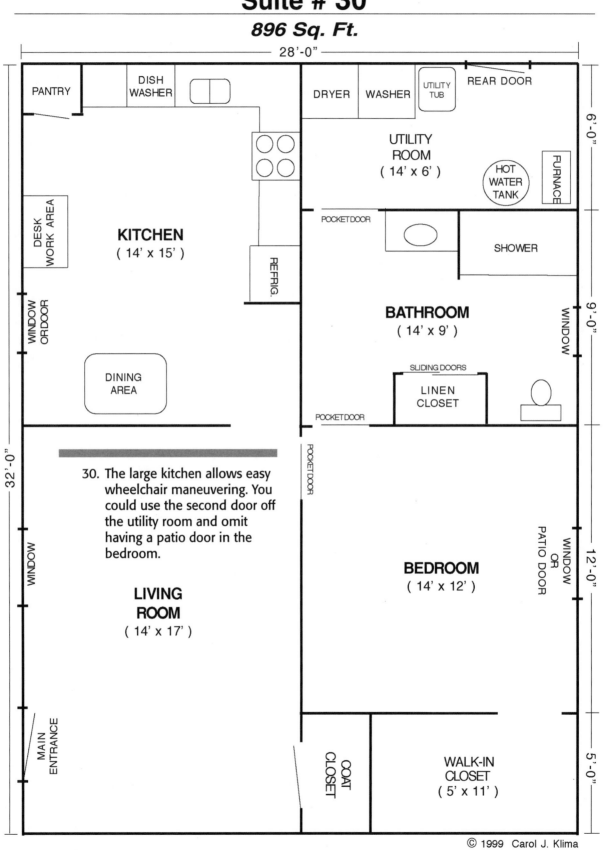

28'-0"

PANTRY

DISH WASHER

DRYER　WASHER　UTILITY TUB　REAR DOOR

UTILITY ROOM (14' x 6')

HOT WATER TANK　FURNACE

6'-0"

DESK WORK AREA

KITCHEN (14' x 15')

POCKET DOOR

SHOWER

WINDOW OR DOOR

BATHROOM (14' x 9')

WINDOW

9'-0"

DINING AREA

SLIDING DOORS

LINEN CLOSET

POCKET DOOR

32'-0"

30. The large kitchen allows easy wheelchair maneuvering. You could use the second door off the utility room and omit having a patio door in the bedroom.

POCKET DOOR

WINDOW

LIVING ROOM (14' x 17')

BEDROOM (14' x 12')

WINDOW OR PATIO DOOR

12'-0"

MAIN ENTRANCE

COAT CLOSET

WALK-IN CLOSET (5' x 11')

5'-0"

REFRIG.

Suite # 30-A
896 Sq. Ft.

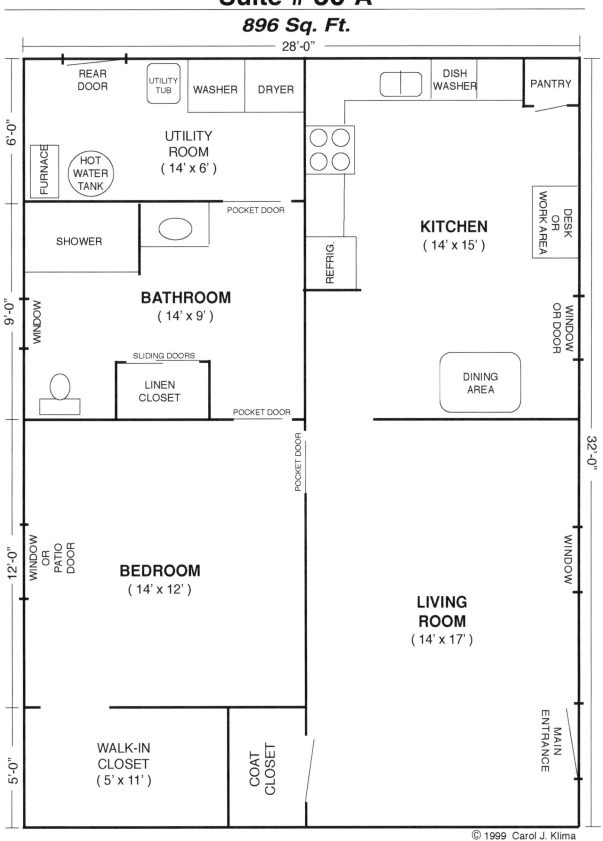

Suite # 31
896 Sq. Ft.

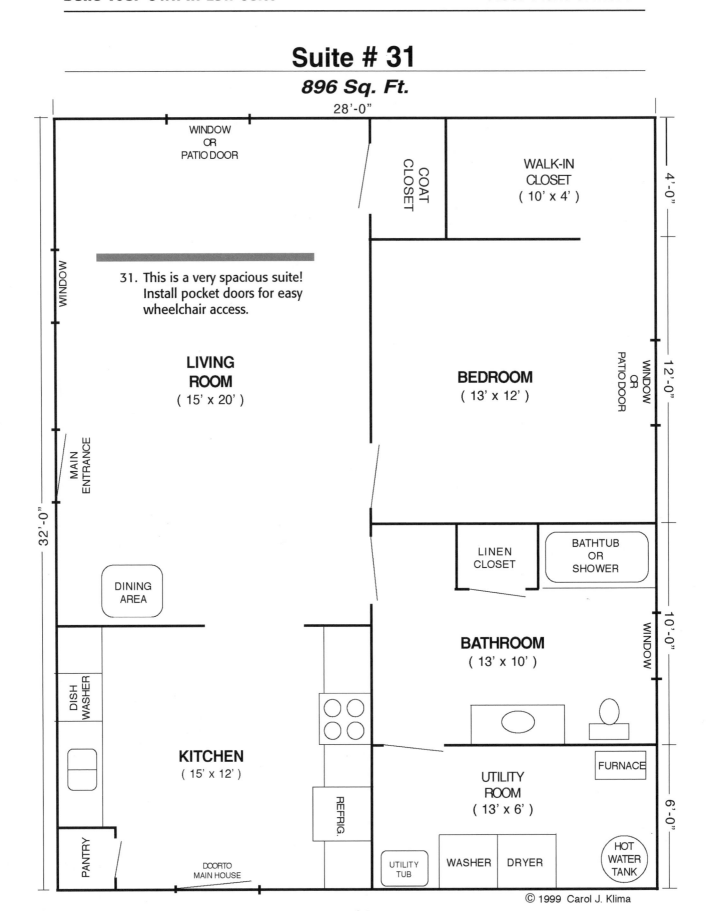

28'-0"

WINDOW OR PATIO DOOR

COAT CLOSET

WALK-IN CLOSET
(10' x 4')

4'-0"

WINDOW

31. This is a very spacious suite! Install pocket doors for easy wheelchair access.

LIVING ROOM
(15' x 20')

BEDROOM
(13' x 12')

WINDOW OR PATIO DOOR

12'-0"

MAIN ENTRANCE

32'-0"

LINEN CLOSET

BATHTUB OR SHOWER

DINING AREA

DISH WASHER

BATHROOM
(13' x 10')

WINDOW

10'-0"

KITCHEN
(15' x 12')

REFRIG.

FURNACE

UTILITY ROOM
(13' x 6')

6'-0"

PANTRY

UTILITY TUB

WASHER

DRYER

HOT WATER TANK

DOOR TO MAIN HOUSE

© 1999 Carol J. Klima

Suite # 31-A
896 Sq. Ft.

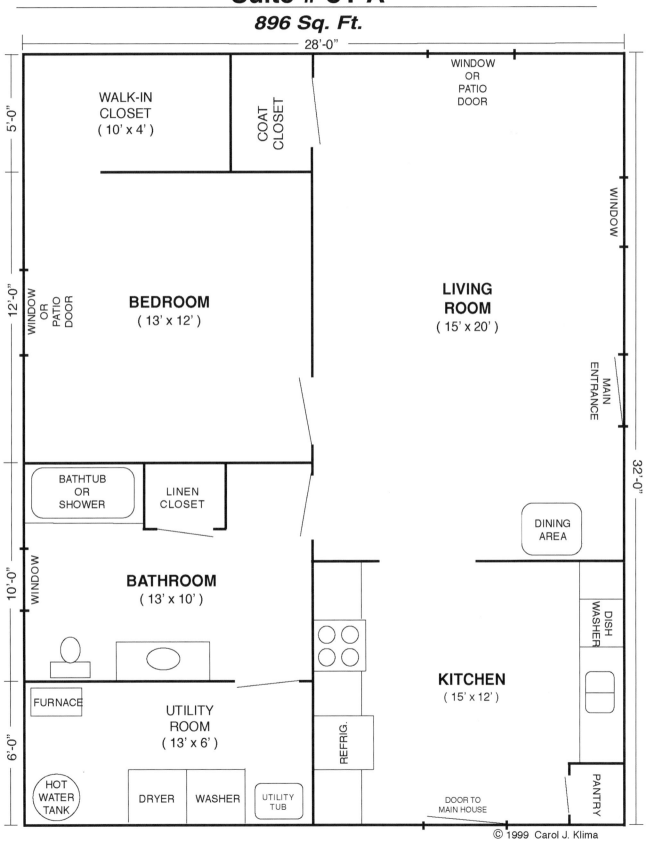

Suite # 32
910 Sq. Ft.

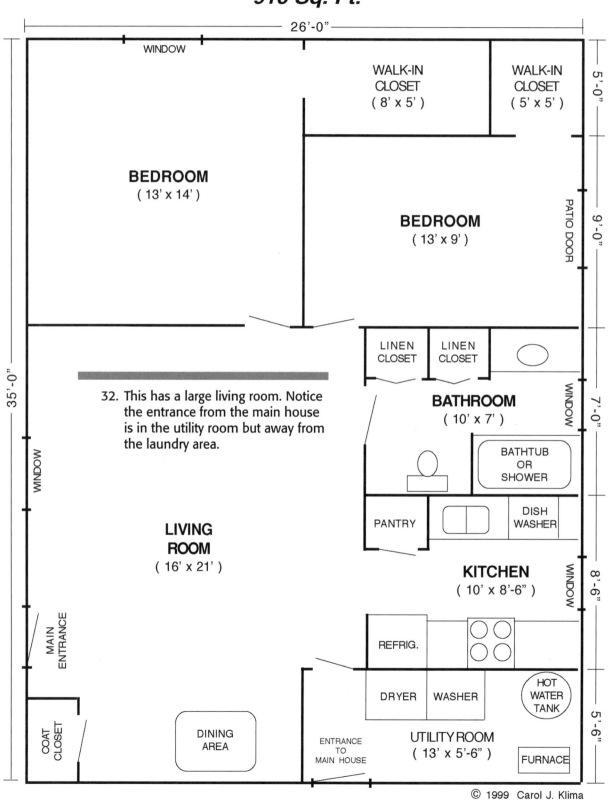

26'-0"

WINDOW

WALK-IN
CLOSET
(8' x 5')

WALK-IN
CLOSET
(5' x 5')

5'-0"

BEDROOM
(13' x 14')

BEDROOM
(13' x 9')

PATIO DOOR

9'-0"

35'-0"

LINEN
CLOSET

LINEN
CLOSET

WINDOW

32. This has a large living room. Notice
the entrance from the main house
is in the utility room but away from
the laundry area.

BATHROOM
(10' x 7')

BATHTUB
OR
SHOWER

7'-0"

WINDOW

PANTRY

DISH
WASHER

LIVING
ROOM
(16' x 21')

KITCHEN
(10' x 8'-6")

WINDOW

8'-6"

REFRIG.

MAIN
ENTRANCE

HOT
WATER
TANK

COAT
CLOSET

DINING
AREA

DRYER

WASHER

5'-6"

ENTRANCE
TO
MAIN HOUSE

UTILITY ROOM
(13' x 5'-6")

FURNACE

© 1999 Carol J. Klima

Suite # 32-A
910 Sq. Ft.

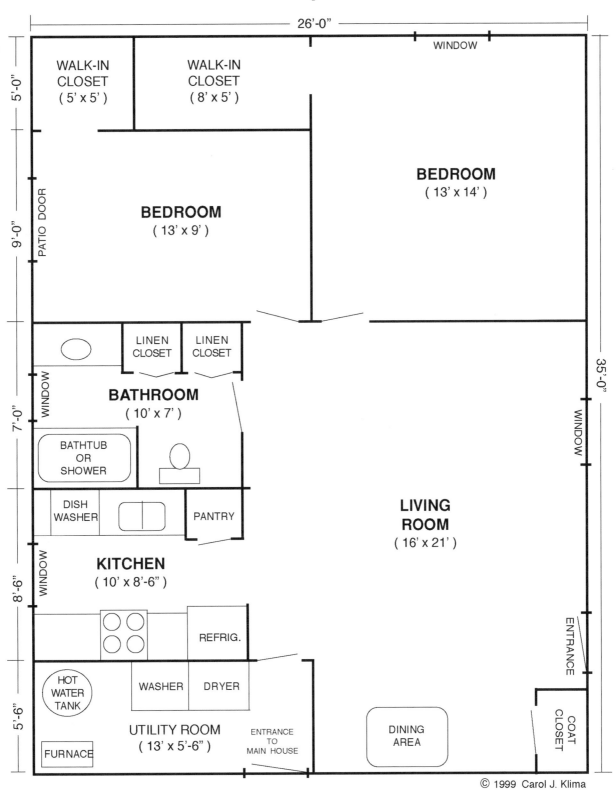

© 1999 Carol J. Klima

Suite # 33
918 Sq. Ft.

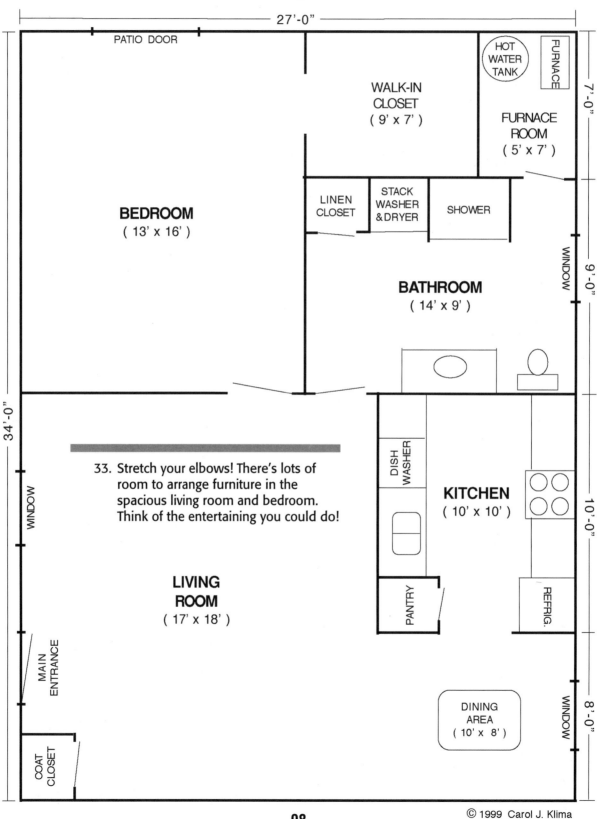

PATIO DOOR

27'-0"

7'-0"

HOT WATER TANK

FURNACE

WALK-IN CLOSET
(9' x 7')

FURNACE ROOM
(5' x 7')

LINEN CLOSET

STACK WASHER & DRYER

SHOWER

BEDROOM
(13' x 16')

WINDOW

9'-0"

BATHROOM
(14' x 9')

34'-0"

33. Stretch your elbows! There's lots of room to arrange furniture in the spacious living room and bedroom. Think of the entertaining you could do!

DISH WASHER

KITCHEN
(10' x 10')

10'-0"

WINDOW

PANTRY

REFRIG.

LIVING ROOM
(17' x 18')

MAIN ENTRANCE

DINING AREA
(10' x 8')

WINDOW

8'-0"

COAT CLOSET

Suite # 33-A
918 Sq. Ft.

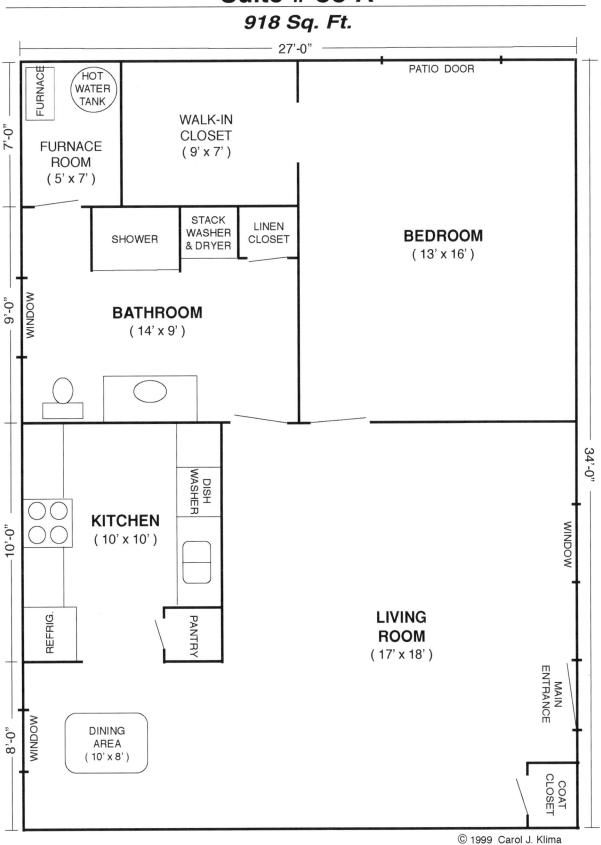

Suite # 34
918 Sq. Ft.

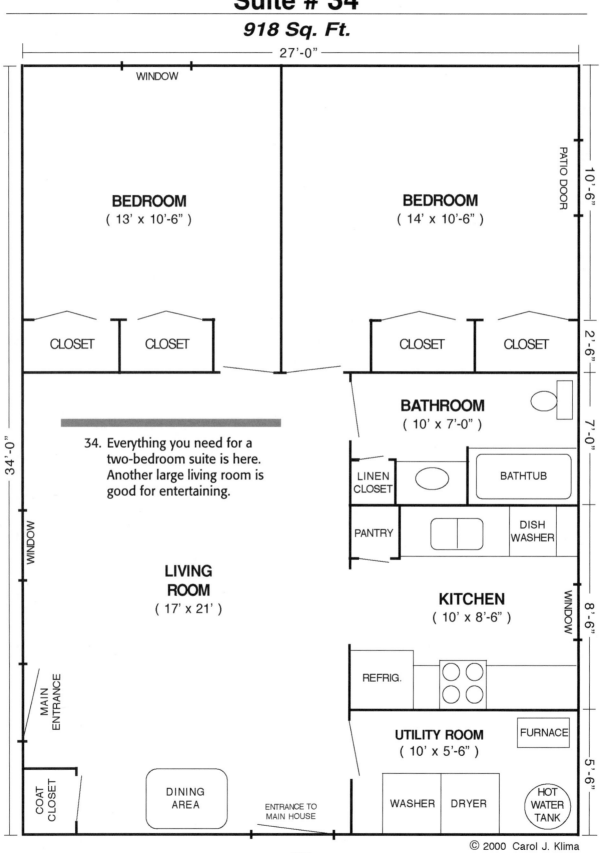

27'-0"

WINDOW

BEDROOM
(13' x 10'-6")

BEDROOM
(14' x 10'-6")

PATIO DOOR

10'-6"

CLOSET   CLOSET

CLOSET   CLOSET

2'-6"

BATHROOM
(10' x 7'-0")

7'-0"

34'-0"

WINDOW

34. Everything you need for a
two-bedroom suite is here.
Another large living room is
good for entertaining.

LINEN
CLOSET

BATHTUB

PANTRY

DISH
WASHER

**LIVING
ROOM**
(17' x 21')

KITCHEN
(10' x 8'-6")

WINDOW

8'-6"

MAIN
ENTRANCE

REFRIG.

UTILITY ROOM
(10' x 5'-6")

FURNACE

COAT
CLOSET

DINING
AREA

ENTRANCE TO
MAIN HOUSE

WASHER   DRYER

HOT
WATER
TANK

5'-6"

© 2000 Carol J. Klima

Suite # 34-A
918 Sq. Ft.

27'-0"

WINDOW

10'-6"

PATIO DOOR

BEDROOM
(14' x 10'-6")

BEDROOM
(13' x 10'-6")

34'-0"

2'-6"

CLOSET   CLOSET

CLOSET   CLOSET

7'-0"

BATHROOM
(10' x 7'-0")

BATHTUB

LINEN CLOSET

DISH WASHER

PANTRY

WINDOW

8'-6"

WINDOW

KITCHEN
(10' x 8'-6")

LIVING ROOM
(17' x 21')

REFRIG.

FURNACE

MAIN ENTRANCE

5'-6"

HOT WATER TANK

DRYER   WASHER

UTILITY ROOM
(10' x 5'-6")

ENTRANCE TO MAIN HOUSE

DINING AREA

COAT CLOSET

Suite # 35
952 Sq. Ft.

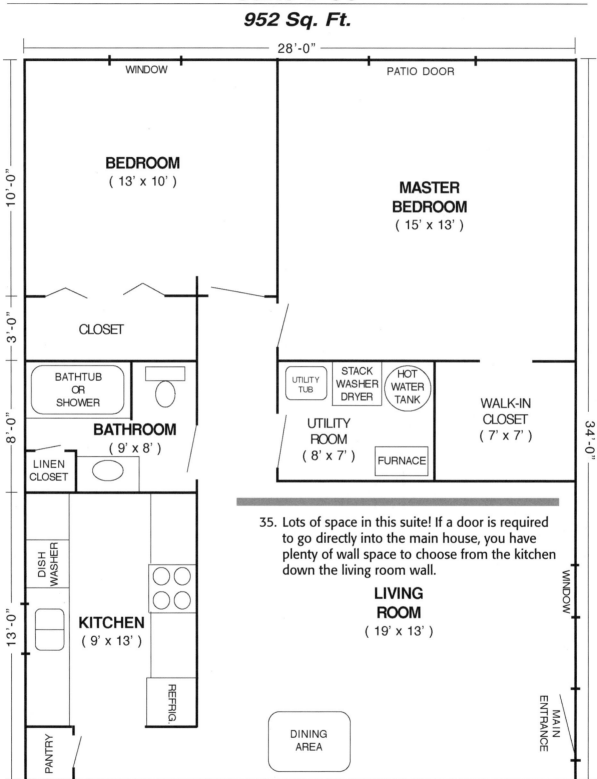

35. Lots of space in this suite! If a door is required to go directly into the main house, you have plenty of wall space to choose from the kitchen down the living room wall.

© 1999 Carol J. Klima

Suite # 35-A
952 Sq. Ft.

28'-0"

PATIO DOOR   WINDOW

MASTER BEDROOM
(15' x 13')

BEDROOM
(13' x 10')

10'-0"

CLOSET

3'-0"

HOT WATER TANK | STACK WASHER DRYER | UTILITY TUB

WALK-IN CLOSET
(7' x 7')

UTILITY ROOM
(8' x 7')

FURNACE

BATHTUB OR SHOWER

BATHROOM
(9' x 8')

LINEN CLOSET

8'-0"

34'-0"

WINDOW

LIVING ROOM
(19' x 13')

DISH WASHER

KITCHEN
(9' x 13')

13'-0"

REFRIG.

MAIN ENTRANCE

DINING AREA

PANTRY

© 1999 Carol J. Klima

Suite # 36
952 Sq. Ft.

28'-0"

WINDOW   PATIO DOOR

WALK-IN
CLOSET
(6' x 6')

BEDROOM
(11' x 12')

BEDROOM
(11' x 13')

15'-6"

BATHROOM
(6' x 6')

LINEN
CLOSET

34'-0"

CLOSET
(6' x 2'-6")

36. A large living room and an
extra half bath are nice when
you have guests.

LINEN
CLOSET

BATHTUB
OR
SHOWER

WINDOW

9'-6"

BATHROOM
(11' x 9'-6")

LIVING
ROOM
(17' x 22')

STACK
WASHER
& DRYER

HOT
WATER
TANK

FURNACE

PANTRY

DISH
WASHER

MAIN
ENTRANCE

WINDOW

9'-0"

KITCHEN
(11' x 9')

COAT
CLOSET

DINING
AREA

REFRIG.

© 1999 Carol J. Klima

Suite # 36-A
952 Sq. Ft.

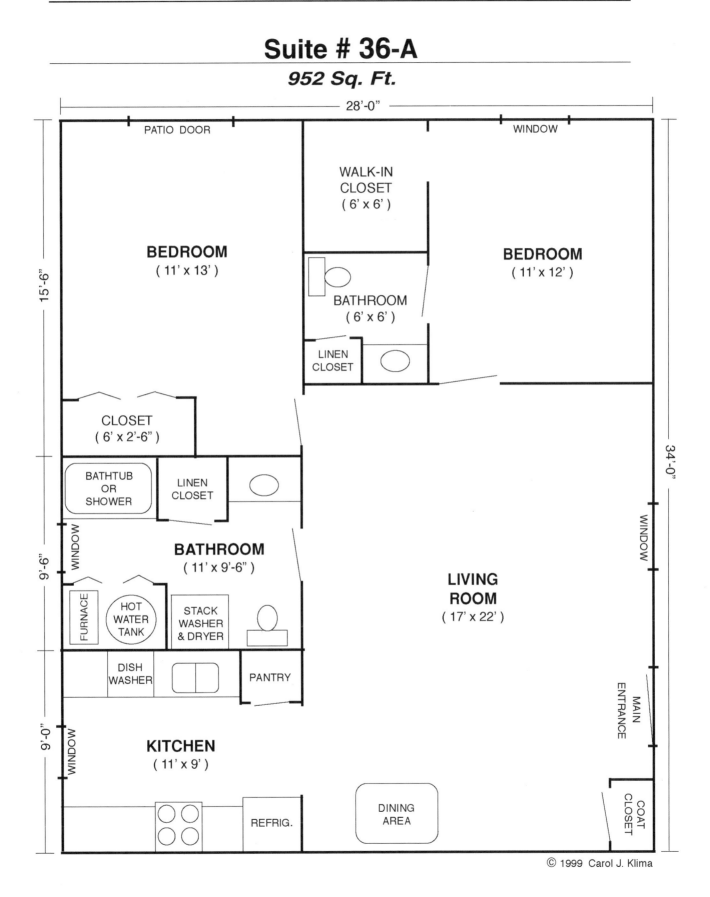

© 1999 Carol J. Klima

Suite # 37
952 Sq. Ft.

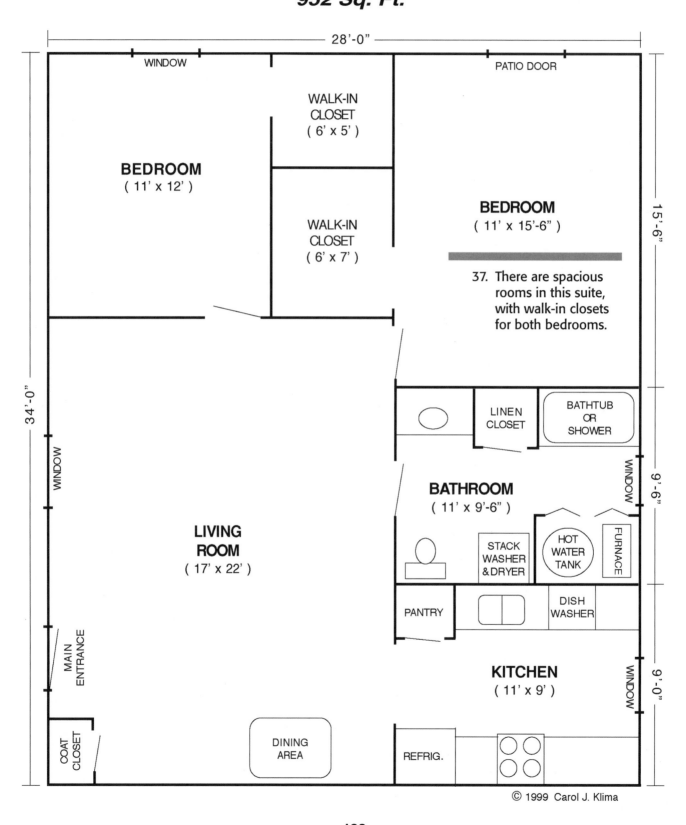

37. There are spacious rooms in this suite, with walk-in closets for both bedrooms.

Suite # 37-A
952 Sq. Ft.

© 1999 Carol J. Klima

Suite # 38
1,008 Sq. Ft.

28'-0"

WINDOW

WALK-IN
CLOSET
(9' x 5')

WALK-IN
CLOSET
(7' x 5')

5'-0"

**MASTER
BEDROOM**
(12' x 15')

BEDROOM
(16' x 10')

PATIO DOOR

10'-0"

36'-0"

LINEN
CLOSET

BATHTUB
OR
SHOWER

38. This has nice large rooms similar
to suite # 24. The wall between
the closets in the bedroom could
be changed to enlarge the other
closet instead.

WINDOW

BATHROOM
(12' x 12')

12'-0"

**LIVING
ROOM**
(16' x 21')

UTILITY
CLOSET

STACK
WASHER
& DRYER

HOT
WATER
TANK

FURNACE

WINDOW

MAIN
ENTRANCE

PANTRY

DISH
WASHER

COAT
CLOSET

DINING
AREA

REFRIG.

KITCHEN
(12' x 9')

WINDOW

9'-0"

Suite # 38-A
1,008 Sq. Ft.

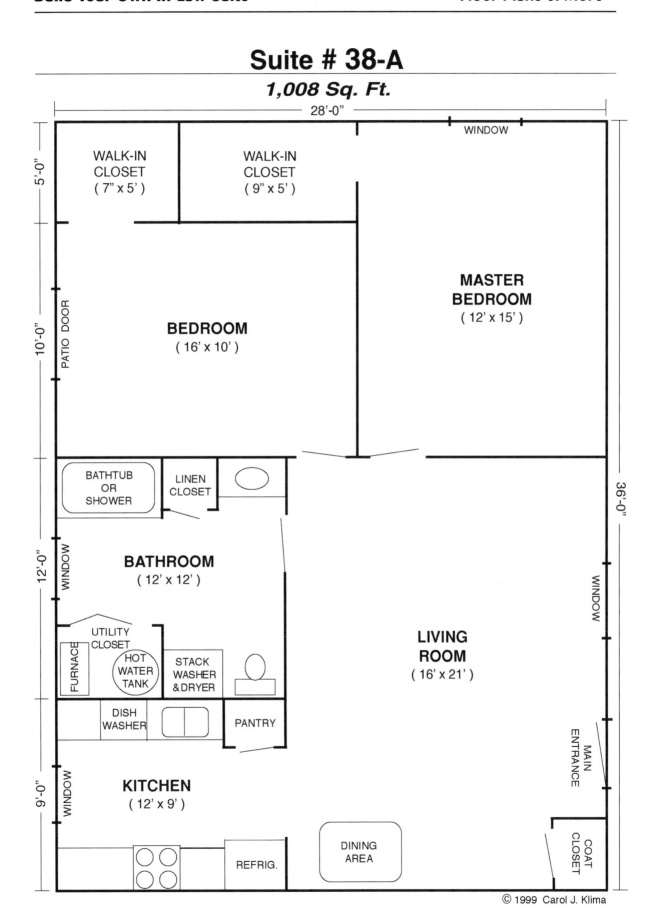

© 1999 Carol J. Klima

Suite # 39
1,064 Sq. Ft.

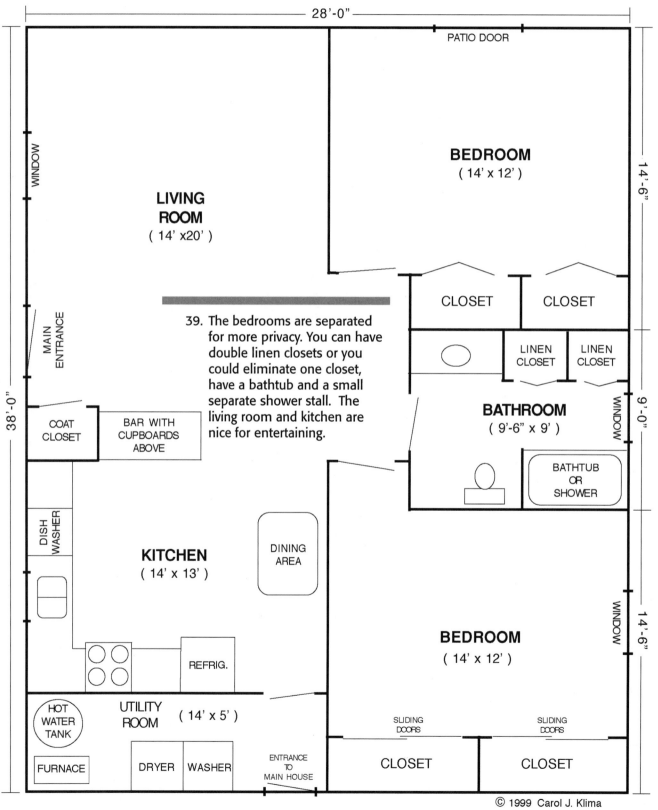

39. The bedrooms are separated for more privacy. You can have double linen closets or you could eliminate one closet, have a bathtub and a small separate shower stall. The living room and kitchen are nice for entertaining.

© 1999 Carol J. Klima

Suite # 39-A
1,064 Sq. Ft.

28'-0"

PATIO DOOR

14'-6"

BEDROOM
(14' x 12')

**LIVING
ROOM**
(14' x 20')

WINDOW

CLOSET   CLOSET

MAIN
ENTRANCE

LINEN
CLOSET   LINEN
CLOSET

9'-0"

WINDOW

BATHROOM
(9'-6" x 9')

38'-0"

BAR WITH
CUPBOARDS
ABOVE

COAT
CLOSET

BATHTUB
OR
SHOWER

DISH
WASHER

DINING
AREA

KITCHEN
(14' x 13')

14'-6"

WINDOW

BEDROOM
(14' x 12')

REFRIG.

SLIDING
DOORS   SLIDING
DOORS

CLOSET   CLOSET

ENTRANCE
TO
MAIN HOUSE

(14' x 5')

**UTILITY
ROOM**

HOT
WATER
TANK

WASHER   DRYER

FURNACE

© 1999 Carol J. Klima

111

Suite # 40
1,064 Sq. Ft.

28'-0"

WINDOW

MAIN ENTRANCE

LIVING ROOM
(14' x 22')

DINING AREA

38'-0"

PANTRY

DISH WASHER

KITCHEN
(9' x 10')

REFRIG.

UTILITY TUB

STACK WASHER & DRYER

UTILITY ROOM
(9' x 6')

HOT WATER TANK

ENTRANCE TO MAIN HOUSE

FURNACE

COAT CLOSET

WALK-IN CLOSET
(10' x 5')

BATHROOM
(6' x 5')

PATIO DOOR

BEDROOM
(14' x 11'-6")

14'-0"

CLOSET

CLOSET

LINEN CLOSET

LINEN CLOSET

WINDOW

8'-0"

BATHROOM
(9'-6" x 8')

BATHTUB OR SHOWER

BEDROOM
(14' x 16')

WINDOW

16'-0"

Suite # 40-A
1,064 Sq. Ft.

28'-0"

14'-0"

8'-0"

16'-0"

38'-0"

PATIO DOOR

BEDROOM
(14' x 11'-6")

LIVING ROOM
(14' x 22')

WINDOW

MAIN ENTRANCE

CLOSET

CLOSET

LINEN CLOSET

LINEN CLOSET

BATHROOM
(9'-6" x 8')

BATHTUB OR SHOWER

DINING AREA

COAT CLOSET

REFRIG.

PANTRY

WALK-IN CLOSET
(10' x 5')

KITCHEN
(9' x 10')

DISH WASHER

BEDROOM
(14' x16')

WINDOW

BATHROOM
(6' x 5')

HOT WATER TANK

UTILITY ROOM
(9' x 6')

UTILITY TUB

FURNACE

ENTRANCE TO MAIN HOUSE

STACK WASHER & DRYER

© 1999 Carol J. Klima

Index

Notes

Notes

Notes

Notes

Notes

Did this book help you?
Or do you have a suggestion of your own?

If you would like to share your experience with me, please send a color shapshot of the suite you built. Add any comments on how this publication helped you, changes you made to customize an in-law suite for your unique situation, any unusual problems, or requirements not mentioned in this book.

Send Comments To:

Homestead Press
Carol J. Klima
396 Fairwood Circle
Berea, OH 44017

888-769-6335

Acknowledgements

Some of the pictures in this publication are from
Hemera Photo Objects®
and Corel Professional Photos®

About the Author

Carol J. Klima is shown here speaking at the NARI Home Improvement Show in Cleveland, Ohio where a walk-thru model suite, built by NARI, was the feature of the show in 2002.

When first considering the option of an in-law suite for her own family, Carol was disappointed to find no suitable publications available to guide her. After going through the step-by-step process of choosing and working with a contractor, she decided to record their family's experience and document her hard-won expertise in a book. She believes there will be a housing shortage for the elderly and that homecare by means of an in-law suite will aid many families to lessen emotional stress and financial burden.

She frequently speaks at community meetings, author events, radio shows, and appears on some television shows, including HGTV's Dream Builders. Between her two books, she has appeared in more than a hundred newspapers, including the Washington Post, Miami Hearld, Chicago Tribune, and the San Franciso examiner.

Carol resides in Berea, Ohio with her husband, a disabled, retired sheet metal worker. The couple have two married children and seven grandchildren. She enjoys playing the piano and reading novels. She loves spending time with her grandchildren as shown on the back cover.

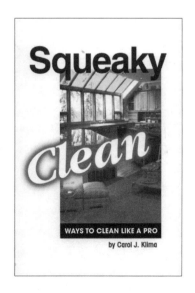

Klima's latest book is *"Squeaky Clean, Ways to Clean Like a Pro."* An easy to read how-to book with step-by-step instructions to become a professional housecleaner, or improve your own home cleaning skills.

Released - October 2002.